Best Hikes With CHILDREN®

in New Jersey

Best Hikes With
CHILDREN™
in New Jersey

By Arline Zatz
and
Joel Zatz

Photographs by
Arline and Joel Zatz

**THE
MOUNTAINEERS**

Published by
The Mountaineers
1001 SW Klickitat Way, Suite 201
Seattle, Washington 98134

First printing 1992, second printing 1994, third printing 1995, fourth printing 1996, fifth printing 1998, sixth printing 1999, seventh printing 2001, eighth printing 2002

Published simultaneously in Great Britain by Cordee, 3a DeMontfort Street, Leicester, England, LE1 7HD

Manufactured in the United States of America
Edited by Meredith Waring
Maps by David A. Zatz
Hikes researched by Joel Zatz
Text written by Arline Zatz
All photographs by Arline Zatz and Joel Zatz
Cover design by Watson Graphics
Typography by Graphics West

Cover photograph: Tripod Rock by Arline Zatz
Frontispiece: Stepping blocks over a stream create a pleasant obstacle for young and old (Hike 41, Loantaka Reservation).

Library of Congress Cataloging in Publication Data
Zatz, Arline.
    Best hikes with children in New Jersey / by Arline
Zatz and Joel Zatz ; photographs by Arline Zatz and
Joel Zatz.
        p.   cm.
    Includes bibliographical references (p. 105-107).
    ISBN 0-89886-272-8
    1. Hiking—New Jersey—Guidebooks.   2. Outdoor recreation for
children—New Jersey—Guidebooks.   3. New Jersey—Guidebooks.
I. Zatz, Joel L., 1935-   .   II. Title.
GV199.42.N5Z38   1992
917.49—dc20   92-24877
                                                                      CIP

Contents

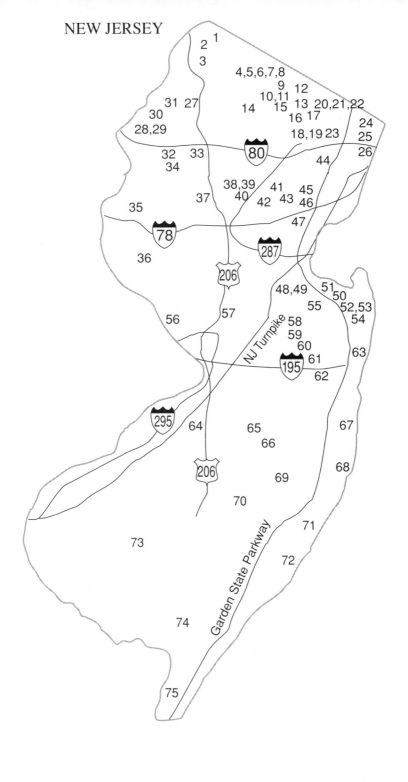

NEW JERSEY

Acknowledgments

We would like to express our sincere appreciation to our son, David, for spending countless hours reading this manuscript, offering helpful suggestions, and designing the trail maps.

Many organizations and individuals supplied valuable information. We owe thanks to the Appalachian Mountain Club; the New York–New Jersey Trail Conference; the Union County Hiking Club; Tom Card, chief ranger at Ringwood State Park; Brian Hardiman, ranger-naturalist at the Delaware Water Gap visitor center; David Hauenstein, public information assistant at the Monmouth County Park System; Tom Koeppel, chief forester at the City of Newark–Pequannock Watershed; Jay Miers, director of Economic Development and Tourism for Warren County; and Paul Tarlowe, senior biologist–information officer for Pequest Trout Hatchery.

Our friends Joyce and Elliot Becker, Rezzan and Metin Celik, Marcia and Seymour Greenwald, Laura and Marvin Mauser, Virginia and Ferris Stoudt, and Mary and Bert Wagner enhanced our scouting expeditions. Together, we learned the importance of always keeping a blaze in sight—particularly just before sunset! We are also grateful for the cooperation and help we received from the editorial staff at The Mountaineers Books: Managing Editor Donna De Shazo, for her infinite patience, wisdom, sense of humor, and West Coast weather reports; Editorial Manager Margaret Foster, for her upbeat attitude; Meredith Waring, copy editor, for carefully editing our manuscript; and Production Manager Marge Mueller for the fine-tuning.

Arline extends heartfelt thanks to Felicia Oliver-Smith, physician extraordinaire, whose encouragement and friendship has brought sunshine on the cloudiest days.

*"Two roads diverged in a wood, and I
I took the one less traveled by,
And that has made all the difference."*

— *Robert Frost*

This book is dedicated to those who blazed the trails for all to enjoy.

Not many can resist tossing a few pebbles into Scarlet Oak Pond (Hike 22, Ramapo Reservation).

Introduction

Webster's Dictionary defines hiking as "a long walk for pleasure in open country." Before we were married, we thought taking a hike meant walking six blocks to the train station. Happily, a few years later, when we figured out that weekends and holidays were times to "get away from it all," we created our own definition of hiking—enjoying the outdoors on foot, while strengthening the heart and employing all the senses.

Why a book on hiking with kids? Simply because hiking with our children has added a lot to our enjoyment of the outdoors. Learning to see nature through their eyes has sharpened our senses and teaching them to appreciate and respect the environment has reminded us to set a good example. When they were younger, they always had a stockpile of questions for us. As a result, we were compelled to read more in order to answer typical inquiries, such as "Why is this called a Christmas fern?" or "How did the boulders get here?" Every adventure resulted in a learning experience for us all.

Many of the hikes we've chosen for this book are those our children have enjoyed through the years, and those we're confident children under twelve can complete with a sense of accomplishment. The hikes were also chosen to appeal to the senses: for the sight of the soothing green of a hemlock grove, the fabulous view into distant valleys, or the sheer variety of shapes found along the trail; for the sound of a churning stream, chirping birds, or the crunch of leaves beneath tiny feet; for the bouquet of fragrant flowers or the pungent aroma of decaying logs; and for the feeling of fresh air on a perspiring face or the smoothness of beech bark on the fingertips. Most hikes in this book can be completed in a few hours, but whenever overnight camping is available, whether it be a tent site, lean-to, or nearby campground, we've mentioned its location.

The Garden State offers hikers great diversity—from the flat, sandy trails in the famous southern Pine Barrens, to the mountainous terrain found in the north. We saw, as you will, New Jersey's hidden gems—the caves, gurgling brooks, waterfalls, and dozens of other examples of Mother Nature's finest work. Whether you opt for an easy hike (which all novices should begin with) or head for a rocky uphill scramble, you'll be guaranteed a rewarding experience. Taking children hiking brings special rewards. Besides the togetherness, you'll discover all kinds of interesting things. Be prepared, however, to stop often; once a child spots a butterfly, a fallen leaf, or an odd-shaped tree, he or she will be reluctant to move on. Relax, take along a hand lens or binoculars, and enjoy the experience together. The way we've found to motivate even the most reluctant child is to provide each with a backpack filled with personal belongings; a small notepad and pencil to encourage a diary of the hike; frequent stops, with promises for some goodies "if they continue moving along"; a friend from time to time, for companionship; and lots of praise. Be patient with them during those unexpected whiny moments or if they fall, and walk at a snail's pace when they get tired.

ABOUT THE HIKES

The hikes are grouped together by locality. A block of information summarizing important details as to the type of hike, difficulty, season hikable, distance round-trip, and elevation gain, is provided at the beginning of each hike. Highlights of each hike, directions for getting to the trailhead and how to proceed, and what to look for along the way, follow.

Hikes range from a little over 1 mile to less than 8 miles. An electronic pedometer was used for measuring distance. Pedometers aren't exact, but one does serve as an additional aid in case a blaze is missing or overlooked. We used the readings to highlight interesting places or plants encountered on the trail. We also used an altimeter and topographic maps to estimate the elevation gain, the difference in height between the highest and lowest points. However, altimeters can be fooled by changes in weather. Another thing to remember is that climbs of successive hills add up, and that continuous ups and downs require more energy than the elevation gain suggests.

HIKE RATINGS

The hikes were assigned ratings of easy, moderate, or difficult (from a child's viewpoint). These have been based on steepness, elevation change, and trail condition. For example, an easy hike indicates flat terrain and good footing, while a moderate hike has some climbs, elevation gain, and/or rough footing in some places. A difficult rating indicates steep climbs, significant elevation gain, and/or a rough trail. Don't hesitate to explore sections of hikes rated moderate or difficult; many have easy sections and feature turnarounds—places within reach that lead to a special view or feature so that children will feel rewarded for the distance hiked.

It's impossible to give approximate times to complete each hike because what may be easy for one person can be more difficult for another. However, 2 mph, plus half an hour for each 1,000 feet of vertical rise, is the usual formula. Also factor in weather, rest stops, lunch breaks, and a child's desire to examine an ant hill or take a dip in a refreshing brook.

TRAIL FOOD

Take along adequate food and drink for the entire outing, plus a bit extra in case of an emergency. Make the food simple, the things children are used to and like. During warm weather, peanut butter and jelly sandwiches won't spoil, but if the kids prefer cold cuts, tuna, or cheese, prechill some individual cartons of fruit juice to keep the food cold. Most kids love peanuts, popcorn, fruit, and raisins; these are all fine snack foods to give them energy boosts. Let them share the planning and they'll love those snack breaks even more!

OUTFITTING

Children (and adults too) are best dressed in layers so that an outer shirt can be removed if it gets too warm or one can be added if it gets chilly. A T-shirt, woolen overshirt, and windbreaker are usually fine for an autumn day, while a down parka or ski jacket would be a good addition for winter. Children love to wear cozy vests under their jackets, too. Remember that fabrics next to the skin have to allow heat to be released and perspiration to be absorbed. Raingear made of new fabrics that repel precipitation but allow perspiration to escape have become popular, although they are much more expensive than more traditional garments.

Pants should always fit loosely. Shorts are fine if you apply sunscreen and are walking in open areas or along the beach, but for most hikes they do not provide enough protection against underbrush, sun, and insects.

While gloves are necessary during cool weather, wearing a hat year-round is strongly recommended. Not only will a hat protect young heads (older ones too) from the sun's hot rays, but it will prevent body heat from escaping during cold weather. A hat can even be worn to bed on an extremely cold night if you're camping. Because a hat is usually one of the first items to disappear on a windy day or when a child bends down to explore a stream, it's a good idea to secure it with a string or to purchase a clip that attaches to the hat and shirt collar.

Bandanas, popular with children, are very useful. Buy a bunch in bright colors and demonstrate how they can be dipped into a stream and used to wash a sweaty face or worn around the neck to cool off. They also can be used as an insect swatter, head covering, pressure bandage, or face mask during a sudden wind, smoke, or hail storm.

Unless otherwise indicated, sneakers will suffice for many of the trips in this book, but when hiking along wet trails, over streams, or in boggy areas, lightweight boots are best. These should be fitted wearing two pairs of socks—a thicker woolen pair over a thin inner pair. Use silicone to keep your boots water resistant. You might also

Long, narrow boardwalks keep your feet dry through the cedar swamp (Hike 1, Monument Trail).

want to consider gaiters, a fabric covering that fits over the top of the boots to prevent water from getting inside. Gaiters are also good protection against ticks, and provide extra warmth.

The Mountaineers has compiled the following list of ten essential items to be taken on all hikes:

1. Extra clothing for changes in weather.
2. Extra food in case the hike takes longer than you planned.

3. Sunglasses to prevent ultraviolet rays from damaging your eyes. Remember to take along a strap to prevent them from falling off when bending down or brushing into a branch.

4. Knife for adults only, unless you're confident younger persons can handle one safely.

5. Fire starter—a candle or chemical fuel, important for starting a fire if you're stuck overnight, but use caution with children around.

6. First-aid kit, which should contain adhesive bandages, gauze pads and tape, antiseptic cream, insect repellent, tweezers, and aspirin.

7. Matches in a waterproof container or a lighter.

8. Flashlight; to prevent arguments, give one to each child.

9. Map.

10. Compass; it's wise to buy one for each child. If they learn how to use it at a young age, they'll never get lost.

Additional items to bring along on the trail should include water in a plastic or metal container holding one quart minimum per person; insect repellent and sunscreen (with a minimum rating of SPF 15); a whistle, in case a child strays from your group (again, give one to each child); toilet paper and a plastic bag in which to carry out human waste (burying it is no longer acceptable); and appropriate medications, especially if your child is allergic to bee or wasp stings. We highly recommend that you purchase, become familiar with, and carry along on all expeditions a copy of the *Emergency/Survival Handbook*, by Robert E. Brown. This book not only contains emergency information, but also includes a reflective centerfold that can be used as a signaling device and a cover that can be used as a fire starter! Lightweight binoculars will enhance any hike, and field guides (see Appendix) can be educational. Many children love taking photographs; you might consider bringing a camera to be shared. Buy each child an album to store memories of past trips and you may end up with another Ansel Adams on your hands!

Sometimes children are reluctant to walk more than a mile or two, but give them a pedometer to keep track of their progress and watch them go! Suggest that they record the miles hiked each trip and add them up at the end of the year. Our sons were so proud of their mileage totals that they bragged about them to all their friends and walked around with ear-to-ear smiles. Remember to reset the pedometer to each child's stride if more than one is using it.

Packs

What about packs? There is an endless selection in packs, from the less costly canvas or nylon rucksack for dayhikes to an internal-frame or external-frame pack for overnight trips. For kids, anything goes, but each child should have his or her own. It's important to get children interested in doing their share, regardless of how much they can tote. Over the years, they'll be willing to carry more and more. Use a fanny pack for the tiny tot in your family for stowing some goodies, an extra sweater, a magnifying glass, or a small canteen, and watch the response!

OVERNIGHT STAYS

Shelter is necessary for overnight trips, and today's hiking family has a wealth of tents to choose from. These range from simple tarps tied onto overhead trees, to lightweight, three-season expedition models for winter trips, to larger, fixed-camp tents. If you're planning on an overnight stay at a lean-to or campground mentioned in this book, there are many how-to-do-it books on the market. (See Recommended Books in the Appendix.)

OUTDOOR MANNERS

Each time we see our sons stuffing candy or food wrappers into their pockets, or cleaning up after a careless hiker, we feel proud to have succeeded in setting a good example. Urge your children to keep the Appalachian Mountain Club's motto in mind: "Carry in, carry out!" Always bring a plastic bag to clean up your debris. For human waste, choose a spot as far away from the trail as possible and at least 250 feet from any water source. (Remember to watch for poison ivy.) Most hikers feel that toilet tissue should be carted out but, at the *very* least, it should be buried 3 to 4 inches deep and the soil placed back carefully. Trail courtesy is a matter of common sense. It's best, even where dogs are permitted, to leave your pet home. Nothing is more annoying or frightening to wildlife or other hikers than a charging, barking dog. Remember, too, that dogs allowed to roam freely can be exposed to poison ivy or ticks, which can then be transferred to humans.

Always stay on the trail so that you don't crush fragile plants or cause erosion and, please, follow the advice "Take only photos; leave only footprints." In this way, others can enjoy the area as much as you did. Should you spot deer or other wildlife, take photographs from a distance so they won't panic. Caution your children to speak in a low voice while on the trail so that they and others can enjoy the sounds as well as sights. It's important to make everyone understand that flowers, pretty moss or lichen, and other natural features on state park or forest land are to be looked at, not picked or destroyed. By using a camera, these precious gifts can be preserved forever. Fireplaces are frequently found along the trail; always check to see if fires are permitted in the area and never cut down live trees for firewood. Be certain to keep the fire small enough to be put out completely before moving on.

WORDS OF CAUTION

Staying on the Trail

Getting lost, even on a short hike, is always a possibility. Stay on the trail; don't try to find the way by straying cross-country. Trails are marked with blazes or cairns. Blazes are usually painted on trees or rocks, with a double blaze indicating a change in direction. Three dots indicate the beginning or end of a trail. Always keep the blaze in view. Should you lose sight of the one in front of you, turn back and find the previous one before continuing. Cairns are piles of stone used to indicate trail direction. Again, always keep the cairn in front of you in view. For an index of USGS topographic maps, which provide more detail than the hiking maps in this book, write to the New Jersey Geological Survey, Map Sales Office, CN 402, Trenton, NJ 08625. These maps highlight all land features and elevations, but aren't updated frequently enough to account for new trails or housing developments that may have destroyed old trails. The New York–New Jersey Trail Conference, 156 Ramapo Valley Road, Mahwah, NJ 07430, also sells waterproof, color topographic maps for a nominal fee.

Poisonous Plants

Be cautious about coming in contact with plants because certain ones can cause severe skin irritation, blisters, and itching. Learn to recognize poison ivy, poison sumac, and poison oak. Poison ivy, which may grow as a plant, bush, or vine on tree trunks, branches, and along riverbanks, has three shiny green leaves ("Leaves of three, let it be") that turn a brilliant red in the fall. Poison sumac, which may grow as a bush or tree, has rows of two pointed leaflets opposite each other and a main leaflet at the top. Poison oak grows in swampy areas as a bush or vine with three leaflets.

You can be poisoned by eating mushrooms found in the woods. Never allow your children to sample anything without knowing absolutely what it is. The Appendix lists several books on first aid and plant identification; it's a good idea to read and discuss this together so that everyone is aware of why it's so important not to nibble along the trail. Water or juices should always be carried in. Because of pollution, caution children never to drink from ponds, streams, or rivers. In an emergency, water from these sources should be boiled for at least 20 minutes, or use iodine tablets or water filtering devices.

Weather

Weather can change at any time, particularly in the northern section of the state at higher elevations. Take the opportunity to study the various cloud formations to predict the likelihood of rain. In 1802,

Luke Howard, an English pharmacist, presented a paper classifying clouds according to basic shapes. Their shapes can indicate fair, stormy, or rainy weather. *Peterson First Guides: Clouds and Weather* (see Recommended Books) is an excellent guide. Many combination pocket barometer/altimeter instruments are available to help predict the weather. A reading below 29.92 inches generally means a storm is brewing close by, while a reading above this is usually an indication of good weather. In case you're stuck in a sudden storm, be aware that young children are particularly susceptible to hypothermia. Carry extra clothing in case the temperature drops and watch for symptoms. The first signs include crankiness and fatigue, while signs of advanced hypothermia include weakness and shivering. Do *not* take shelter under the tallest tree during a lightning storm; if you're on a ridge, leave immediately. Also, remove your pack if it has a metal frame. If you're caught in the midst of a lightning storm, the American Hiking Society suggests you "find a grove of trees, a space between two boulders, or any low spot. Sit or crouch. Do not lie down."

Insects, Snakes, Bears, Rabid Animals

Mosquitos and black flies are pests, but Lyme disease is a serious problem in New Jersey. While the tick that carries this disease can be found right on your own front lawn, it is more common in the Pine Barrens in the southern part of the state. Wearing long-sleeved shirts and long pants, tucking pants legs into socks, or wearing gaiters can be a big help. Help your child check his or her body after each walk in case any ticks have hopped aboard. The tick responsible for spreading this disease is remarkably tiny, about the size of a poppy seed. Experts recommend wearing light-colored clothing and white socks so that a hitchhiking tick will be easy to spot. Tick repellent can be used, but it's most important to make frequent self-inspections. If a tick has adhered to your skin or your child's, gently use tweezers to remove it.

Black bears have frequently been found in the northern part of the state. While they are dangerous, they'll smell you coming before you can spot them and will probably run for cover. If a bear should head toward you, make lots of noise, blow your whistle, or bang stones against a metal canteen. It's important to keep your cool because a bear can outrun you. If all else fails, walk backward slowly and climb the nearest tree. If you're out in the open, the American Hiking Society suggests playing dead. "Protect your belly, neck, and inside of your arms and legs by clasping your hands tightly behind your neck and lying face down with your legs pressed together." They also warn if the bear rolls you around to "try to stay curled in the fetal position. Don't struggle, cry out, or resist." If you're tenting overnight, don't leave food in the tent; suspend all food and garbage in sealed bags

The old-fashioned water pump at the beginning of the Three Mountain Ponds trail is just the ticket on a hot day (Hike 31, Three Mountain Ponds).

at least 12 feet off the ground.

New Jersey is experiencing an increasing number of rabid animals. It's wise to stay away from even the cutest raccoon or squirrel. Don't let your children grope inside holes in logs or rocks, and learn to identify poisonous and nonpoisonous snakes.

Hunting Season

Wear bright colors during hunting season. Hunting isn't allowed on Sunday, but check with local parks or the New Jersey Department of Environmental Protection for dates it is permitted.

Theft

One final caution. It's a fact of life that thieves operate all over, even at deserted trailheads and campsites. Try to leave all valuables at home, and leave nothing inside the car to tempt a thief looking for a good day's haul.

We've listed some possible hazards, but if you use common sense, you'll find that hiking with kids is fun, free, and fulfilling.

Lao-tzu remarked that "The longest journey starts with just one step." Go outdoors with your family, take that first step onto one of these suggested hiking trails, and we promise you'll be on your way to an exciting journey. Enjoy!

Key to Symbols

 Dayhikes. These are hikes that can be completed in a single day. While some trips allow camping, only a few require it.

 Backpack trips. These are hikes whose length or difficulty makes camping out either necessary or recommended for most families.

 Easy trails. These are relatively short, smooth, gentle trails suitable for small children or first-time hikers.

 Moderate trails. Most of these are 2 to 4 miles total distance and feature more than 500 feet of elevation gain. The trail may be rough and uneven. Hikers should wear lug-soled boots and be sure to carry the Ten Essentials.

 Difficult trails. These are often rough, with considerable elevation gain or distance to travel. They are suitable for older or experienced children. Lug-soled boots and the Ten Essentials are standard equipment.

 Hikable. The best times of year to hike each trail are indicated by the following symbols: flower—spring; sun—summer; leaf—fall; snowflake—winter.

 Driving directions. These paragraphs tell you how to get to the trailheads.

 Turnarounds. These are places, mostly along moderate trails, where families can cut their hike short yet still have a satisfying outing. Turnarounds usually offer picnic opportunities, views, or special natural attractions.

 Cautions. These mark potential hazards—cliffs, stream or highway crossing, and the like—where close supervision of children is strongly recommended.

Legend

Parking for hike 🚗
Other parking area P
Campground/tent site ⛺
Scenic overlook 📷
Tree 🌲
Picnic area ⚒
Trail blaze color Ⓖ

Trail blaze colors:
    O = orange
    G = green
    R = red
    B = blue
    W = white
    P = pink
    N = brown
    S = silver

Features:
■ Manmade point of interest
● Natural point of interest
━ Dam or dike
＼ Power lines
＼ Gate
⌒ Swamp or marsh
＼ Fence
▦ Bridge

A NOTE ABOUT SAFETY

Safety is an important concern in all outdoor activities. No guidebook can alert you to every hazard or anticipate the limitations of every reader. Therefore, the descriptions of roads, trails, routes, and natural features in this book are not representations that a particular place or excursion will be safe for your party. When you follow any of the routes described in this book, you assume responsibility for your own safety. Under normal conditions, such excursions require the usual attention to traffic, road and trail conditions, weather, terrain, the capabilities of your party, and other factors. Keeping informed on current conditions and exercising common sense are the keys to a safe, enjoyable outing.

The Mountaineers

On a clear day you can see almost forever from atop the ridge at High Point.

1. Monument Trail

Type:	Dayhike
Difficulty:	Moderate for children
Distance:	4.9 miles, round trip
Elevation gain:	300 feet
Hikable:	Year-round
Hours:	Dawn to dusk
Information:	High Point State Park, 1480 State Route 23, Sussex 07461; (973) 875-4800
Admission:	Fee for parking, Memorial Day to Labor Day

You can see forever (or almost forever) if you hike through High Point State Park on a clear day. The road leads to a parking lot beside a 220-foot obelisk built in memory of New Jersey's wartime heroes. It stands 1,803 feet above sea level—the highest point in New Jersey.

The 291-step climb to the top is definitely worth the effort, but save those vistas for the end of the hike. If you're too tired by the time you get to the monument, the view from the base is also fine for admiring the Delaware River, the Pocono and Catskill mountains, the Wallkill River Valley, and various farms. The trail, a series of mini ups and downs along the Kittatinny Mountain Ridge in the northwestern corner of the state, passes through dense woods and a cedar swamp and along the bank of Lake Marcia, the highest lake in the state. Bring along a magnifying glass to examine the sphagnum moss in the swamp and binoculars to view the hawks and vultures that frequent this area.

Campsites, wooden tent platforms, and cabins are available at the Sawmill Lake Camping area within the park.

From Colesville, in the northwest corner of the state, take NJ-23 north into High Point State Park. Just past the park office on the left, turn right and follow signs to the monument.

Long pants are a good idea; where the trail narrows, you'll be brushing against shrubbery. Walk away from the monument to the far end of the parking lot onto the Monument Trail, which is designated by a red and green circular blaze. The narrow, level trail is rocky, with a mixture of pitch pine, oak, and beech towering overhead. As you begin a gradual climb at 0.2 mile, look to the left for an exceptional view of the Delaware River and Pennsylvania. For the remainder of

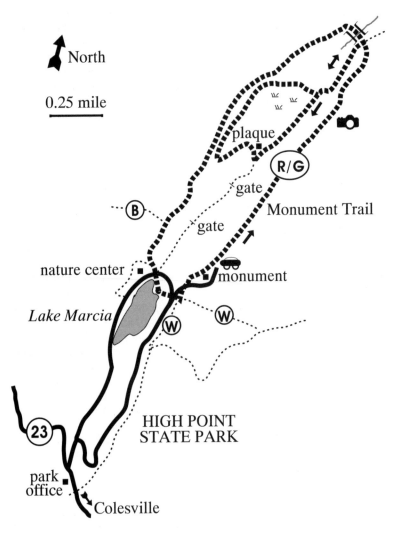

North

0.25 mile

plaque

R/G

gate

B

Monument Trail

gate

nature center

monument

Lake Marcia

W

W

HIGH POINT
STATE PARK

23

park
office

Colesville

the hike, you'll be encountering slight ups and downs until the last segment, which is steep.

Fall is grand; besides the color change, you can watch the squirrels scurrying about looking for acorns. As you descend at about 0.3 mile, some of the rocks on the trail are on a vertical tilt, making it a bit difficult to negotiate. A few yards ahead, you'll be crossing over a sea of boulders beneath beautiful red maple and mitten-shaped sassafras. Continue to the ridge at 0.5 mile, and turn right onto a short, narrow path leading to an overlook with an exceptional view.

When ready to proceed, return the way you came, again watching where you place your feet as you descend steeply into the woods. When the trail levels and you reach the wooden bridge at 0.9 mile, turn left onto a wide, level road, which is closed to traffic, and walk slightly uphill. In a few yards, you'll encounter easy ups and downs, as well as stands of tall rhododendron, some reaching 15 feet high. At the trail junction at 1.2 miles, follow the left fork into the cedar swamp. Soon, at 1.5 miles, you'll enter an area with lush ferns that turn a brilliant yellow in fall. At the next road junction, just ahead, turn right. As you do, you'll find a memorial plaque dedicating this natural area to John Dryden Kuser. Avid birdwatchers, Colonel Kuser and his wife donated this land to provide a nature reserve open to the public that would help conserve clean water. They also provided funds to build the obelisk.

You'll find beautiful cedars in the swamp ahead, as well as many beeches and chestnut oaks. Then the trail starts narrowing again, and if you look to the right at just under 2 miles you'll see sphagnum moss in the boggy area. A careful search may turn up the carnivorous sundew and pitcher plants. At 2.1 miles, trees have sprouted up through the cracks in the boulders. Continue along the narrow boardwalk through a very wet area covered with sphagnum moss and the unusual wild calla plant, which is filled with red berries in fall. This is a great area to take out the magnifying glass, lie on the boardwalk, and study the interesting plants below. At the T where you originally entered the cedar swamp, turn left, and if you didn't notice the rhododendron the first time, you'll have another opportunity. Turn left when you reach Monument Trail again and cross over the wooden bridge. The trail begins to climb steeply at 3 miles and the Delaware River appears to the right.

In about 0.25 mile, you'll be descending through a mixed-wood forest along a narrow path, and for a while there'll be some dips and rises, until 3.9 miles, where the trail ascends steeply. Stone steps have been placed every so often, making walking easier. On windy days, the trees have a melody of their own as the limbs scrape each other and the leaves shake in the breeze. After huffing and puffing a bit, you'll see the monument to the left through the trees at about 4 miles. At the road junction, turn left and follow the road. Use caution; an occasional car may come by. In a few yards, after descending slightly, Lake Marcia appears on the right.

If you'd like to pause for a snack, pick a boulder for a natural chair. Continue on the Monument Trail, ascending steeply over boulders. Watch your footing; some are loose. Cross the road, watching for cars, and cut through the woods again, but don't venture too far without having a blaze in sight. When the foliage is dense, they're difficult to see. The trail continues uphill through the woods, crossing a road again before reaching the monument. At this point, you can climb the stairs to the top (fee) or admire the surrounding country-side from the base before continuing to the nearby parking area.

---

2. Above Lake Rutherford

Type:	Dayhike
Difficulty:	Difficult for children
Distance:	5.2 miles, round trip
Elevation gain:	250 feet
Hikable:	Year-round
Hours:	Dawn to dusk
Information:	High Point State Park, 1480 State Route 23, Sussex 07641; (973) 875-4800
Admission:	Fee for parking Memorial Day to Labor Day; permit necessary for overnight camping

Wear sturdy shoes—you'll need them to negotiate thousands of rocks while exploring the southern portion of High Point State Park. The struggle along this section of the Appalachian Trail is worth the

Groundhogs are often spotted in High Point State Park.

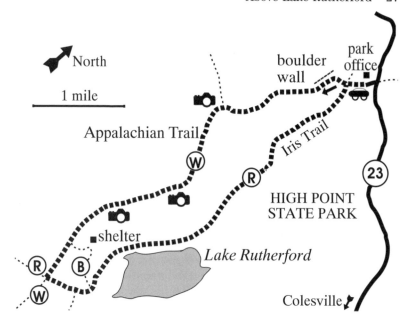

effort, because the views along the crest of the Kittatinny Mountains are sensational. If you come during July or August, plump blueberries are yours for the picking, but be certain to identify what goes into your mouth; there are some look-alikes that may be poisonous. In early morning or late afternoon, there's a good chance of spotting a groundhog as it makes its way along the rocky slopes in search of tender plants to eat. According to folklore dating from the sixteenth century, should the groundhog be frightened by its shadow when emerging from hibernation on February 2, it will head back under-ground, and spring will be delayed for another six weeks.

The park office is located on NJ-23, just west of Colesville, in the northwest corner of the state. Free brochures are available. To reach the trail, turn right and drive east on NJ-23, making the first right onto a dirt road that leads directly to an unpaved trail parking lot.

Facing the office, enter a narrow trail located between two stone blocks, then turn left onto a trail marked by both white and yellow blazes. In 0.1 mile, you'll see a red marker and a sign on the left indicating the terminus of the Iris Trail, while the yellow trail takes off to the right. Continue straight ahead, following the white blazes of the Appalachian Trail as it gradually climbs. At the T at 0.25 mile, in front of a wall of granite, turn left. From here, you'll be going up and down over rocks and boulders of all sizes and shapes. There's a lovely view of forest and mountain ridges to the west with Sawmill Pond in the foreground, at just over 1 mile.

The trail then turns eastward, leaving the ridgetop. You'll descend on loose rocks that resemble a river of boulders, and then scramble up again on a similar bed of granite. A steep rock outcrop appears shortly and, when you sit down to rest, check out the show. At your feet, ants scurry about every which way, carrying loads of food that weigh more than they do. In spring, tent caterpillars are busy building their cotton candy-like webs, while the larva of the small spotted-winged fly has formed around the brown galls on many twigs. Another 0.5 mile brings you to an overlook facing east, with a view of Lake Rutherford. In a few yards, the view is even better; here, you'll see why New Jersey is nicknamed the "Garden State." The well-marked trail meanders along on high ground, finally reaching a ledge with another beautiful vista to the east; use caution because there's a sharp dropoff. A short distance farther, a sign and blue blazes indicate the way to an overnight shelter. Turn back the way you came and enjoy the vistas again on the way to your car.

If you'd like to lengthen the trip (by about a mile) and return by a different trail, continue south on the Appalachian Trail until you cross the Iris Trail, marked with red blazes. Turn left, following the Iris Trail past Lake Rutherford and eventually back to the start.

3. Culver Tower

Type:	Dayhike or overnight backpack
Difficulty:	Difficult for children
Distance:	4.5 miles, round trip
Elevation gain:	600 feet
Hikable:	Year-round
Hours:	Dawn to dusk
Information:	Stokes State Forest, 1 Coursen Road, Branchville 07826; (973) 948-3820
Admission:	Free

In the first century A.D., Publius Syrus wrote the maxim, "A rolling stone gathers no moss." Perhaps he was inspired by hiking trails similar to those in Stokes State Forest, where thousands of odd-shaped rocks are adorned with lush, green moss. You'll have a fabulous view of Pennsylvania and the Delaware Water Gap from the mountain ridge traversed by the Appalachian Trail. Nearby stands the Culver Fire Tower, which is only manned when the risk of fires is high. Kids can

The view of the surrounding countryside from Culver Tower is extraordinary.

rarely resist the temptation to climb the six flights of stairs leading to the top, but caution them to hold onto the railing; the winds are quite strong at this altitude.

In autumn this is a great place to watch the bird migration, so bring binoculars and a bird identification book. As you meander through a small portion of the 15,000 acres that make up Stokes State Forest, you'll see a great variety of trees and wildflowers. There are also two camping areas where you can stay overnight.

From Newton take NJ-206 north. Turn right on Coursen Road into Stokes State Forest, drive past the park office, take the next right, and continue for a short distance to the Stony Lake day-use area.

Sturdy shoes are recommended for negotiating the rocky trail because sneakers will not protect small feet from sharp rocks encountered along the way.

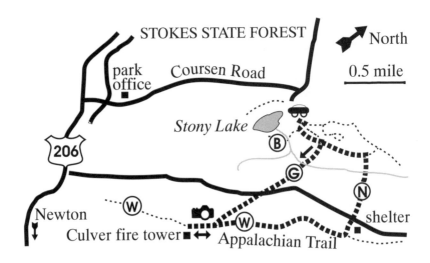

At the far end of the parking lot, toward the stone fence, look for a bulletin board with a trail map. Just behind this is a wide gravel path with a metal barrier. Take this path, which leads gradually uphill past light green, dark green, brown, and blue blazes. At the trail junction, follow the green, brown, and blue markings. Chestnut oaks form a thick canopy overhead and, as the trail descends slightly at 0.2 mile, continue straight on the dark green- and brown-blazed trail when the blue trail veers off to the right. An impressive hemlock grove soon appears.

Where the trail levels, a stone wall will be on the left. This once served as a boundary marker. At 0.5 mile, turn right, following the green-blazed Tower Trail, but watch your footing; rocks pop up everywhere. Lots of scrub oak and fern, along with moss-covered rocks, are found along this narrow section of trail. As the trail ascends steeply at 0.7 mile, you'll probably spot lots of salamanders darting for cover at the sound of your footsteps.

Use caution crossing the road at 1.2 miles and while climbing the natural rock staircases. An open view to the west soon unfolds, a preview of the magnificent vista at the crest of the ridge. Pay attention on this narrow, rocky section; there are some steep dropoff areas. The rocks can also be quite slippery after rain or early morning dew. The top of the ridge (1.5 miles) is a fine place to look out upon the Gap and surrounding farms, to view soaring vultures and hawks, or to relax and have lunch. Turn right onto the white-blazed Appalachian Trail, and walk 0.1 mile to the Culver Fire Tower. Hikers can climb the steps for a a spectacular 360-degree panorama, but hold on to the railing in case there's a sudden gust of wind.

Turn around, heading north now on the Appalachian Trail, and go past the junction with the Tower Trail. Follow this narrow, level path that has occasional views to the west. Turn left at the brown blazes at 2.8 miles, descending on the now wider but still rocky trail, which leads past a shelter. Stay with the brown blazes identifying the Stony Brook Trail. After crossing the road, head steeply downhill using Mother Nature's rocks and tree roots to gain sure footing. Cross the stream at 3.1 miles, where considerate hikers have placed rocks to protect against wet feet, and continue on to a wider section of trail fairly free of rocks. The trail is now less steep, with occasional ups and downs. Moss and lichens thrive in the shaded, damp forest, and a lovely grove of evergreens appears at 3.9 miles, with the scent of pine disappearing all too soon. The Stony Brook Trail also comes to an end. Turn left onto the wide, level Station Trail and follow it back to the Stony Lake area.

4. Laurel Pond

Type:	Dayhike
Difficulty:	Moderate for children
Distance:	4 miles, round trip
Elevation gain:	220 feet
Hikable:	Year-round
Hours:	Dawn to dusk
Information:	Wawayanda State Park, P.O. Box 198, Highland Lakes 07422; (973) 853-4462
Admission:	Free, Memorial Day to Labor Day

This is black bear territory, but have no fear; they'll scamper off as soon as they smell you. With the plentiful supply of berries and acorns these dense woods offer, the black bear grows from its birth weight of 1 pound to 300 pounds! Don't feel cheated if you don't spot any because there's lots more to enjoy while hiking the beautiful trails within Wawayanda State Park. For openers, at the beginning of the hike there's a fantastic view of Wawayanda Lake, a crystal-clear body of water covering 255 acres. You'll also see the remains of an iron furnace over 40 feet high built in the nineteenth century; a cedar swamp; and Laurel Pond, which is spring-fed. If you're here during warm weather, plan on taking a refreshing dip at the end of the hike.

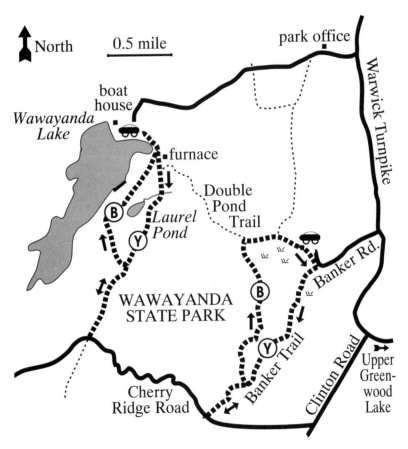

North   0.5 mile

park office

Warwick Turnpike

boat house

Wawayanda Lake

furnace

Double Pond Trail

B

Laurel Pond

Y

Banker Rd.

WAWAYANDA STATE PARK

B

Banker Trail

Y

Clinton Road

Upper Greenwood Lake

Cherry Ridge Road

Or relax on the sandy beach and watch sailboats and canoes drift by while fishermen wait patiently for a bite.

Enter Wawayanda State Park on Warwick Turnpike north of Upper Greenwood Lake. Drive to the boathouse and park.

Facing the lake, walk to your left along the shore. When you reach a trail with blue markings, walk straight ahead, going slightly uphill. Bear left at the fork; just past the end of the lake, in about 0.25 mile, are the remains of a charcoal blast furnace built by Oliver Ames and his sons in 1846. The initials "W.L.A," which his son, William, etched on the lintel on the main arch—along with the date—are still visible, but ivy is slowly obscuring it. Iron ore was fired here at temperatures of 2,000 degrees F., and the finished products, known as "pigs," were used to make shovels and railroad car wheels. Swords were added to the list during the Civil War.

In another 0.1 mile, cross a bridge bearing three yellow blazes on the right post; this identifies the Laurel Pond Trail. The pond, adorned with an abundant supply of cattails, is home to bullfrogs. In springtime, the males sing their courting songs loud and clear to attract a mate. The southeast portion supports an impressive stand of hemlock, thought to be the only virgin timber on the mountain. Bear tracks have been reported in this pristine area. Continuing uphill, you'll see huge boulders hugging the side of the trail, as well as shimmering silver pussy willows bursting open in early spring. In about 0.5 mile, you'll have a great overall view of the pond.

Stands of hemlock and rhododendron dot the hillside, adding a touch of color to the grayish rock formations. At just under 1 mile, you'll be on a dirt path with a gully to your left and towering hemlocks to your right. The aptly named Wingdam Trail, marked in blue, enters shortly thereafter. At this point, turn right into the woods to return or continue on the yellow trail. You'll be walking with a rocky outcrop to your right and the gully to your left as you head downhill. You may want to take a break to look over the magnificient boulder field not far ahead. Once you enter hemlock territory, at about 1.5 miles, the forest seems even quieter than before. Only an occasional chipmunk rummaging through the fallen leaves or a chickadee singing from a nearby tree breaks the hush.

The Laurel Pond Trail ends at an intersection with Cherry Ridge Road, a wide dirt path. Turn around here and head back, keeping an eye out for the blue markings that appear in about 0.75 mile. There is a double yellow blaze at the junction. Turn left, following the blue

Iron furnace built in the nineteenth century

blazes uphill. Club moss abounds in between the massive boulders. Be careful as you step across the irregular-shaped rocks up ahead. Soon, the trail levels off and becomes fairly free of obstructions. If you're here during early spring, you'll hear the almost deafening high-pitched cry of the spring peeper, a small treefrog found only in the north and identified by an "X" on its back.

A few yards ahead is one of the highlights of this hike: a large dam where water topples over giant boulders on its way into Wawayanda Lake. Continue downhill; in about 0.25 mile you'll be at the lakeshore once again. Turn left and follow the water's edge back to the start. By this time, you'll have seen why the Lenape Indians called it Wawayanda, which means "water on the mountain."

5. Cedar Swamp

Type:	Dayhike
Difficulty:	Easy for children
Distance:	3.9 miles, round trip
Elevation gain:	100 feet
Hikable:	Year-round
Hours:	Dawn to dusk
Information:	Wawayanda State Park, P.O. Box 198, Highland Lakes 07422; (973) 853-4462
Admission:	Free

It's almost impossible to get lost because huge rhododendron thickets form a natural fence along this trail. Sporting leathery dark green leaves throughout the year, with large pinkish-purplish flowers from late spring to early summer, these towering beauties also provide an ideal hiding place for wildlife. Here in Wawayanda Park, children and adults can appreciate and learn about the outdoors. Bring a sturdy bag so that little ones can collect interesting leaf specimens found along the trail, and encourage them to recognize the difference in tree shapes, perhaps starting with an oak and a hemlock. Paper and crayons are great for making rubbings. When you find tree bark with an interesting texture, or see a leaf with an interesting shape, place a piece of paper over it, rub it with a crayon, and you'll have a permanent record.

Although the rhododendron are glorious, you'll also pass through

This reindeer-shaped tree is excellent for making a rubbing as well as to look at.

a white cedar swamp, and will find sphagnum moss, hear bird calls, see frogs, and much more. Waterproof shoes are a good idea because sections of the trail may be wet or muddy.

From the junction of Warwick Turnpike and Clinton Road at the south end of Upper Greenwood Lake, follow Warwick Turnpike north for about 1 mile and turn left onto Banker Road. When the pavement ends, turn right onto the dirt road and follow it to the end. Park along the side of the road.

Walk back on the dirt road the way you drove in. Before the blacktop road begins, in front of a horse farm at 0.2 mile, turn right onto Banker Trail, a wide dirt path with yellow blazes. In a few yards, a pond will appear on the left. Beware of the lush poison ivy here. Continue straight; cross the boardwalk and the short bridge over a swampy area that leads to a wet, heavily wooded area where rhododendron and hemlock make their first appearances. It's so junglelike in here that the sun never has a chance to shine through the brush. Watch out for the hundreds of tree roots that crisscross the trail in about 0.3 mile, and in another 0.1 mile, look for a huge bowl-shaped depression on the left. If you're here during late summer when the oaks are shedding their acorns, stop for a minute or two to listen to them hitting the ground. Hopefully, your head won't be in the way! Children are usually delighted to learn acorns make great whistles. All they have to do is place both thumbs over the cap, leaving a tiny slit, and blow through the cavity to create a high-pitched sound.

Be on the lookout for a right turn at about 0.75 mile. The trail soon climbs for a short distance, takes a slight dip, levels out before a steep 0.1-mile climb, and finally levels out again. The rhododendron suddenly disappear at this point, replaced by graceful green hemlocks. Ahead, at 1.5 miles, swaying phragmites announce the swampy area and, in a short distance, a T and a tree with three yellow blazes mark the end of Banker Trail. Turn back the way you came. In about 0.4 mile, look for impressive stands of rhododendron appearing on both sides of the trail, just before the start of the blue-blazed Cedar Swamp Trail. Turn left, following the blue markings.

Gradually climbing beneath a canopy of beech and hemlock are many young trees that have sprouted between boulders split by winter's constant freezing and thawing. Continue along this beautiful wide trail, which, when it levels at 2.3 miles, is shaded by unbelievably high rhododendron. A large swamp appears 0.1 mile later; thanks to the efforts of considerate hikers, rocks and logs have been placed over most of the wet area, which is covered with sphagnum moss. As you round the bend a short distance ahead, keep an eye open for an old oak with a strange, gnarled trunk on the right. If you see large droppings on the trail, look for large paw prints as well. These belong to the black bear. They'll usually do everything they can to avoid you as soon as they catch your scent.

Walking over the long, meandering boardwalk that skirts through the cedar swamp, you can view dozens of plants with heart-shaped leaves, called water arum or wild calla. In early summer, lovely masses of greenish white unfold from the leaves; in late summer, the masses ripen into red berries. When you reach the end of the Cedar Swamp Trail at 3.4 miles, make a sharp right turn heading east. A single yellow marker identifies the trail to Double Pond Road, and on the remaining 0.5 mile back to your car, you may encounter some wet areas where deer gather to quench their thirst.

6. Surprise Lake

Type: Dayhike
Difficulty: Difficult for children
Distance: 3.5 miles, round trip
Elevation gain: 650 feet
Hikable: Year-round
Hours: Dawn to dusk
Information: A. S. Hewitt State Park,
c/o Wawayanda Park Box 198,
Highland Lakes 07422;
(973) 853-4462
Admission: Free

Just about everything a hiker could want can be found on this hike. For openers, there are fabulous vistas of Greenwood Lake, which, stretched out like a long finger, extends from New Jersey into New York State. The lake was created when German industrialist Peter Hasenclever lived up to his name, building a dam at nearby Long Pond to provide power for the Ringwood ironworks. Today, the lake is jam-packed with boaters and fishermen. Although the trails on this hike are strewn with boulders and walking can be a bit difficult at times,

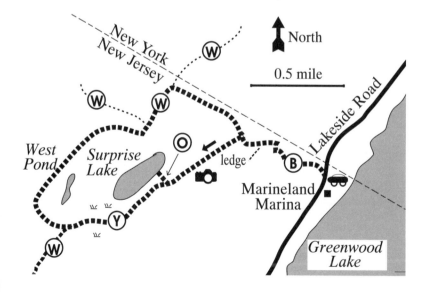

A hiker can be "king of the mountain" atop the ridge over-looking Greenwood Lake on the way to Surprise Lake.

there are plenty of opportunities for rest breaks. Besides the lake, you'll pass a tiny pond and a small stream and walk under dark canopies of mature rhododendron.

Sturdy shoes are recommended for negotiating the rocky trails, and use caution when walking on the ridges because the surface is uneven in many places.

This hike begins on the western shore of Greenwood Lake within a few feet of New York's border. Drive north from West Milford alongside the lake (on Lakeside Road), and park on the right side at the sign announcing entry into New York.

Walk south 0.1 mile, turn right into the parking lot opposite MarineLand Marina, and look for a double blue marker on a tree. Turn left, following the blue blazes of the State Line Trail as you cross the gully, continuing slightly uphill with the stream to the left. From this point, you'll have numerous minor ups and downs—and a few steep areas—while meandering through deep woods. In nearly 0.5 mile, you'll be climbing up a sea of boulders. After a heavy rain, tiny waterfalls drop down between these rocks, but you won't get your feet wet because there are lots of rocks to walk on.

Markings aren't tightly spaced, so don't get too far ahead without making certain you're still on the trail. As you climb steeply, you'll have a first-hand look at the many white streaks of quartz in the rocks. In a short distance, you'll reach a horizontal wall of rock where many trees have sprung up through the cracks. A blue blaze appears at about 0.7 mile and, a few feet farther, a double white square blaze painted on a boulder. At this point, you can detour about 10 minutes for a great view of Greenwood Lake by turning left and walking along the ridge. After enjoying the view and observing the hawks, walk back to the rock ledge where you originally saw the double white square blaze and continue, climbing gradually. Turn left onto the yellow-blazed Ernest Walter Trail at about 1 mile. Proceed uphill, steeply in places, over the boulders. The trail becomes so narrow in another 0.2 mile that the blueberry bushes seem to reach out and grab you. In a few feet, you'll reach another view of Greenwood Lake, even more exceptional than the first. This is a good spot to rest, have a snack, and get the feeling of being "king of the mountain." It's easy to be in touch with nature atop the ridge while watching others below water-skiing and boating.

When ready, continue ahead on the rock face. Usually there are hawks floating effortlessly overhead. Just when you think you've seen the prettiest view of the lake and surrounding countryside, there's an even better one ahead. From this viewpoint, you'll see an island smack in the middle of the lake on the New Jersey side. Look for the yellow blaze a short distance ahead and follow it into the woods, heading downhill on a narrow path. When you reach a triple orange blaze, turn right to Surprise Lake; the surprise is that you'll probably be all alone! Return to the yellow trail, which leads to a steep natural rock staircase and marvelous 15- to 20-foot-tall stands of rhododendron. Climbing down, you'll know what it feels like to be in a funnel because the trail seems to disappear in front of your eyes. Soft, damp moss covers the boulders, resembling the best carpet money can buy. The trail soon levels out and suddenly, at 1.5 miles, you enter almost total darkness—another short stretch of rhododendron has overgrown the trail, providing a thick canopy. Where boulders accumulate 0.2 mile ahead is often where feet begin to ache. These angular chunks of rock have frozen and thawed so many times that they've cracked; that's also why so many are standing sharply on end.

After crossing a bridge of boulders over a swampy area, climb steeply uphill on the bare rock face. White blazes appear at the top; stay on the yellow trail leading into the woods. After a couple of minor ups and downs, you'll have to hold on to rocks and tree limbs once again to make it down into a narrow valley of rocks; sometimes a sitting position works best. The reward—and a fine place to catch your breath—is in a small glen. This low point is wonderfully peaceful. Not many hikers can resist tossing leaves into the small stream or wetting bare feet.

Look to the right for a view of West Pond when you reach the mountain ridge. The yellow trail ends at about 2.5 miles at a junction with the Appalachian Trail (white blazes). Head right, immediately climbing toward the edge of the ridge where there's an unobstructed view of the surrounding mountains. Turn right when you reach the blue blazes of the State Line Trail a short distance ahead. Continue following the blue markings down, back to the parking lot, and return to your car.

7. Shepherd Lake

Type:	Dayhike
Difficulty:	Moderate for children
Distance:	5 miles, round trip
Elevation gain:	350 feet
Hikable:	Year-round
Hours:	Dawn to dusk
Information:	Ringwood State Park, Box 1304, Ringwood 07456; (973) 962-7031 or (973) 962-7047
Admission:	Free; parking fee Memorial Day to Labor Day

Shepherd Lake, a 74-acre spring-fed lake located in the heart of the Ramapo Mountains, is only one of the delights seen on this hike. While meandering through a tiny section of Ringwood State Park you'll encounter lots of wildlife. You'll also be within walking distance of

Skylands Manor House, a reproduction of the Jacobean mansions built in the English countryside 400 years ago, and Skylands, the state's official botanical garden.

One of the many wildflowers to be found along the trail is the bright red columbine, identified by five long, narrow spurs on a slender stem. Look up and you'll see tall, stately oak, maple, and beech. Look down and chances are you'll spot a rabbit or raccoon.

Plan on being on the trail early in the day; if the weather's warm, you may opt for a refreshing swim after the hike. Or, if you want to fish, trout, largemouth bass, sunfish, and pickerel are plentiful; a license is required.

This impressive eagle guards the entrance to Skylands and the beginning of the hike.

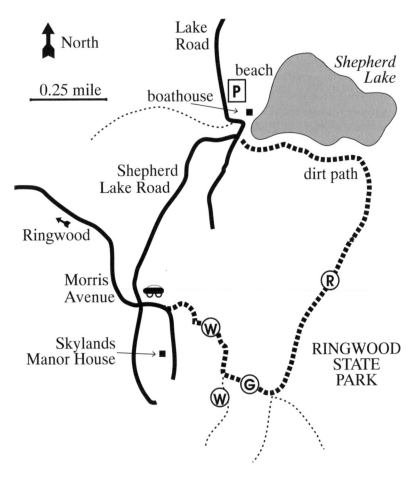

 From NJ-511 in the town of Ringwood, head north toward Ringwood State Park. Turn right on Morris Avenue and continue to the Skylands section of the park. Park in the A parking area, on the left side of the road.

After leaving the parking area, walk left onto the entrance road, heading east, and look for white blazes leading to the left. Rows of crab apple trees, a feast for the eyes when they bloom in spring, appear on the right at 0.1 mile. Follow the white blazes, and turn left onto a grassy path that leads beneath a canopy of magnolias. You'll hear the music of a babbling brook before you see it on the left at 0.3 mile.

In a few feet, turn left at the triple green-on-white blaze. In spring, it seems that dozens of white violets pop up along this narrow, rocky trail. Wanaque Reservoir is visible to the right at 0.6 mile. In this next stretch look for columbine in the crevices. Growing to a height of 2 feet or more, this pretty wildflower bears a beautiful five-petaled flower that grows like a lantern, face down, from March to April. Ancient herbalists used the juice of this plant to cure stomachaches.

The trail levels at the top of the ridge at 0.9 mile. Double red-and-green blazes signal a trail junction. Turn left onto the red trail. A huge rock wall is to your left where the trail levels, with marvelous vistas ahead. This is a good area to sit to enjoy a snack or simply admire the rolling hills and countryside.

After a steep descent at about 1.4 miles, the trail levels and leads to an area with large boulders, perfect for sitting or climbing on. After a few ups and downs, the trail levels again and becomes very narrow at 1.8 miles. At 2 miles, white birch appear and, in another 0.25 mile, Shepherd Lake comes into view. Turn left and follow the dirt path along the lakeshore. Skunk cabbage, one of the first plants to poke up through the snow, abounds in this wet area.

At 2.5 miles, you'll be opposite the boathouse and picnic area. This is a good spot to watch the boaters and fishermen, or perhaps join them. A fine swimming beach is also nearby. After enjoying the scenery and activities at the lake, retrace your steps back to Skylands and your car.

8. Governor Mountain

Type:	Dayhike
Difficulty:	Moderate for children
Distance:	2.3 miles, round trip
Elevation gain:	200 feet
Hikable:	Year-round
Hours:	Dawn to dusk
Information:	Ringwood State Park, Box 1304, Ringwood 07456; (973) 962-7031
Admission:	Free

No matter which season you choose to hike to the top of Governor Mountain, you'll have an exhilarating view of the countryside from what locals refer to as "Suicide Ledge." Added rewards include a bountiful carpet of wildflowers during spring and towering red cedars. Sturdy hiking shoes are recommended for negotiating the steeper sections of trail.

From Ringwood, take Ringwood Avenue (NJ-511) north, bear right on Sloatsburg Road, and turn right again on Carletondale Road. Park in the Community Presbyterian Church parking lot on the right, about 0.5 mile down the road; ask permission to leave your car there.

Walk left (west) on Carletondale Road. Turn left onto the yellow-blazed Cooper Union Trail just past a fire hydrant (which faces large boulders on the opposite side of the road). Each fall, the beeches, oaks, and maples towering overhead put on a show of vibrant yellows, browns, and reds. If the trees have already shed their leaves, watch out for holes between the rocks that may be covered.

In a few yards, you'll reach a tree with a split trunk. From this point, proceed slightly uphill, crossing over the small stream. Children like to test their balancing skills on the narrow boards that have been placed here and, inevitably, one or two "accidentally" fall in.

The narrow, rocky trail continues to gradually ascend through dense hemlock stands until the fork at 0.3 mile, where you'll bear right. A series of ups and downs follow before leveling 0.2 mile later. After another climb, you'll reach a swampy area at 0.7 mile, a good place to create a game of hopping-over-the-rocks to avoid getting wet. In about another 0.1 mile is an enormous fallen tree that's large enough to support ten adults or twenty children.

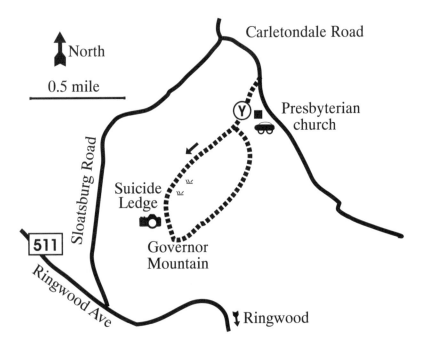

Views of the surrounding countryside and the reservoir are exceptional from the trail.

The ascent is steeper as you pass beautiful red cedars on the left. You'll probably see cedar waxwings munching on the tree's luscious berries. The trail soon levels and, at about 1 mile, you'll have a magnificient view of Wanaque Reservoir. This huge, clear body of water has the capacity to supply several towns with 100 million gallons of water daily.

From this point, the trail descends steeply to the right, toward the reservoir; be careful on the loose rocks. Another great view of the reservoir and countryside, and a good place to stop for lunch, is at Suicide Ledge, named for its straight drop.

When ready, continue along the edge of the ledge past large boulders. Use caution because this section can be slippery. In a few yards, head briefly uphill; the trail then descends steeply. Some of the smaller boulders in this area may also be slippery, so use care and go slowly. The most difficult part of the hike is now over. As you follow the trail through the woods, take time to observe the thick carpet of moss at 1.4 miles, as well as the huge boulders and ironwood trees scattered here and there.

The huge boulder (a glacial erratic deposited here by an ice sheet around 12,000 years ago) encountered at 1.7 miles is a perfect challenge for children, who can't resist climbing it. After passing this beauty, continue downhill steeply. Stay right at the trail junction, taking the original trail past the tree trunk shaped like a tuning fork, back to the starting point.

9. Terrace Pond

Type:	Dayhike
Difficulty:	Moderate for children; difficult if alternate is taken
Distance:	5–5.5 miles, round trip
Elevation gain:	340 feet
Hikable:	Year-round; peak wildflower bloom May–June
Hours:	Dawn to dusk
Information:	Newark Watershed Conservation Development Corporation (NWCDC), Echo Lake Road, Newfoundland 07435; (973) 697-2850
Admission:	Permit necessary (contact NWCDC)

Getting to Terrace Pond is half the fun of this hike, but be forewarned: Kids can't resist stopping dozens of times along the way to launch leaf boats down a brook, climb huge boulders, or admire the tiny waterfall. At several points along the trail, you'll have a good chance of finding the rare pink lady's slipper. Hold out for lunch until you reach a granite ledge overlooking the pond, where you can eat while gazing down upon this sparkling jewel. Plan on starting out early so you can spend lots of time enjoying Terrace Pond, which, in our opinion, is one of the loveliest places in northern New Jersey. Although the trail is easy most of the way, sturdy shoes are recommended for negotiating a few of the rocky, sometimes slippery, areas.

 From NJ-23 in Newfoundland, drive 6 miles north on Clinton Road to a small parking area on the right (east) side of the road (across from a row of large rocks).

The trail begins a few yards south of the parking area. Follow a wide, unmarked, rocky road that heads east and take the first woods road to the left at about 0.3 mile. Continue uphill another 0.2 mile and bear right at the Y onto a wide trail with yellow blazes, the Terrace Pond South Trail. Observe this intersection carefully, as you'll be returning the same way. There should be a cairn (column of rocks) to mark this junction. The trail in this area is wide and level and many of the surrounding trees have been defoliated by gypsy moths. With a magnifying glass, you can examine their egg cases left on the limbs

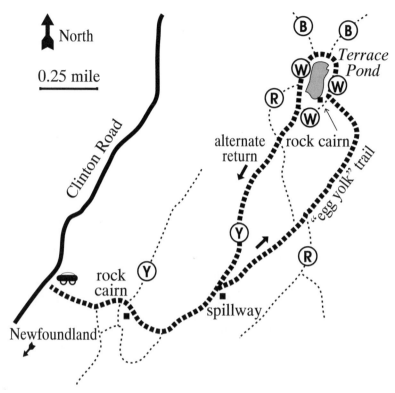

and tree trunks or, in early spring, you can watch as thousands of gypsy moths emerge from each egg case.

The spillways at the 1-mile point are good spots to linger for a moment. A few yards ahead huge boulders form a wall on the right. Here, a new trail with a blaze resembling an egg yolk—a yellow circle on a white background—appears. Take this trail; gradually, you'll climb past more rock walls.

At 2 miles, turn left and begin carefully climbing up the ridge. (There's a sharp dropoff on the left where the trail narrows.) Follow the trail as it turns left and reaches its highest point atop a rocky ledge at 2.2 miles. Here you'll feel "on top of the world" as the wind blows through your hair. Turn right onto the white trail, indicated by blazes on the rocks. Continue descending steeply for 0.3 mile to the pond. It's possible to explore the shoreline by following the trail that encircles the pond.

To return, you can retrace your steps, but be careful not to miss the beginning of the egg yolk trail at 2.6 miles; it's marked by a rock cairn on top of the boulders, with three egg yolk blazes a few feet behind. Another rock cairn at 4.5 miles signals the intersection with

Hikers have Terrace Pond to themselves year-round.

the unmarked woods trail that you took on the way in. Continue straight ahead on this trail at the cairn instead of following the yellow trail to the right. Then turn right again to the starting point.

A recommended alternative is to circle the pond and take another route back partway. This is longer by about 0.5 mile and also more strenuous, but the views and local scenery make the extra strain worthwhile. Follow the white trail as it circles the pond in a counterclockwise direction. Blue markings soon join in. The walking is wet in spots and there are some boulders to clamber over. Beautiful stands of mountain laurel set off views of the pond. Stay to the left as blue blazes head off to the right, and continue following the pond. About 0.5 mile from the start of the return trip, the Terrace Pond South Trail with its yellow blazes begins. Follow this southward as it leads over several ridges and finally brings you to the junction with the egg yolk trail. Continue for about 0.6 mile, keeping an eye out for the cairn identifying the unmarked trail you came in on. Continue straight as the yellow markings turn right, then turn right at the T to the starting point.

10. Buckabear Pond

Type:	Dayhike
Difficulty:	Moderate for children
Distance:	4.6 miles, round trip
Elevation gain:	200 feet
Hikable:	Year-round
Hours:	Dawn to dusk
Information:	Newark Watershed Conservation Development Corporation (NWCDC), Echo Lake Road, Newfoundland 07435; (973) 697-2850
Admission:	Permit necessary (contact NWCDC)

Early afternoon is the best time to enjoy exquisite views of Clinton Reservoir and the final destination, Buckabear Pond. Don't be afraid to try this hike during winter, when the slightest breeze pushes thin layers of ice toward the shore, creating melodious sounds. Attractions, in addition to a refreshing hike through a variety of trees, include an abundance of birds, lush mountain laurel, flowing brooks, and evidence of beaver activity. Wear sturdy shoes to avoid stubbing your toes on this extremely rocky trail. You may wish to bring along a tree identification book. Trail maps can be obtained at the Pequannock Watershed on Echo Lake Road, off NJ-23 south of Clinton Road. A special permit (fee), required before parking in the watershed area, should be obtained at the same office.

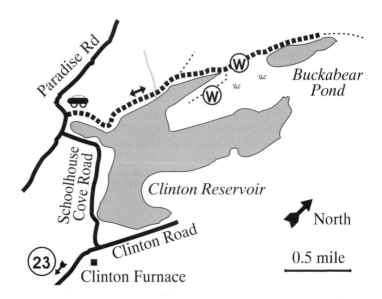

 From NJ-23, north of Newfoundland, take Clinton Road north 1.2 miles and turn left onto unmarked Schoolhouse Cove Road. (The remains of Clinton Furnace are off the right side of Clinton Road just before the turn.) Continue 1 mile, turn right onto another dirt road, and drive 0.1 mile to the parking lot on the right.

To begin, head gradually uphill from a tree marked with three white blazes to the left of the parking area. Clinton Reservoir soon comes into view. Continue along its rim until the double white blaze at 0.25 mile and follow the blazes, which lead along the water's edge. Distinctive ironwood trees thrive in the moist, shady areas and can be identified by their twisting gray-and-blue-banded trunks and, in spring, by drooping clusters of stiff bracts. The tree with the yellowish sheen on its peeling bark is the yellow birch; its seed cones provide a steady diet for birds in winter.

At 0.75 mile, just before the trail descends, look to the right for a tiny island shaded by evergreens. A brook crosses the trail in a few yards, and if the temperature is right, it's a fun spot to pick icicles. If not, the sound of the tumbling water provides free entertainment. The trail now levels for a few yards before beginning a series of dips and climbs. At a trail marked by three white blazes, stick to the right, heading along the edge of the reservoir. You may have to head off into the brush for a short distance at a couple of low spots around 1.4 miles to avoid large puddles. Check out the trees along the water's edge just after this section. You may see beavers; fresh chips at the base of a tree are a dead giveaway they're around, as are the branches they've gathered to block the water.

Continue walking along the water's edge. What looks like the remains of a rusty tractor appears at about 2.3 miles and just ahead is the perfect spot to admire Buckabear Pond. A wide, flat boulder provides a natural seat for a picnic lunch or a rest. Turn back after enjoying the view.

Beavers are very much alive and well in this area—and quite fond of certain trees!

11. Bearfort Mountain Lookout

Type: Dayhike
Difficulty: Moderate for children
Distance: 6 miles, round trip
Elevation gain: 300 feet
Hikable: Year-round
Hours: Seasonal; subject to change
Information: Newark Watershed Conservation Development Corporation (NWCDC), Echo Lake Road, Newfoundland 07435; (973) 697-2850
Admission: Permit necessary (contact NWCDC)

The destination of this hike is the fire tower, where a panoramic view of the countryside more than makes up for the absence of bears. When climbing to the top platform, hold on to little ones who may get excited and lose their footing on the steep steps. Wear sturdy hiking shoes to assure a firm grip over the countless boulders.

The hike, a joy in any season, is extra special in the spring, when the wildflowers and azalea bloom, and in the fall, when Mother Nature paints the leaves in brilliant colors. One note of warning: Several trails intersect this area; those that are marked use only white blazes, so be alert at each junction. It's a good idea to have a compass handy. Trail maps can be obtained at the Pequannock Watershed on Echo Lake Road, off NJ-23 south of Clinton Road. A special permit (fee), required before parking in the watershed area, should be obtained at the same office.

From NJ-23 in Newfoundland, take Clinton Road north for 2 miles. Park on the right at a small cutout bordered by two huge boulders.

The beginning of the trail is unmarked. Go past a gate and head north, uphill, on a wide, rocky path flanked on the right by a stream. In about 0.25 mile, on the right, you'll find stone steps and a stone wall. Let the kids limber up by running up and down the steps while you figure out what this foundation was built for. Once back on the main trail, continue straight ahead to the first white blaze. This is a densely wooded area where there is shade on even the hottest summer's day. After the pond on the right, the trail curves left and leads to an open area. Cross this section, head left, and at the Y at

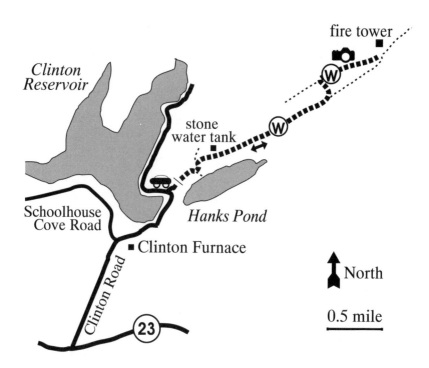

0.6 mile, bear right. In a few yards on the left there will be a large stone structure. If you look for an entrance, you won't find one. That's because it's a water tank. Built in the late 1800s, it supplied water via a pipe and springhouse to a castle farther south belonging to New York clothing manufacturer Richard Cross. The castle was disassembled a few years ago.

Ahead are giant boulders perfect for climbing. This spot is a favorite hangout of woodpeckers and songbirds. A gradual climb begins at 0.9 mile, and after some level areas the trail gets steep for about 0.25 mile. Soon, you'll be walking atop boulders, and at 1.5 miles there may be a tiny waterfall formed by the runoff from a swampy area.

You'll face a challenge a few yards ahead at a glacially formed rock outcrop. It's fun to explore, but be careful, because the rock can be slippery and the narrow ledge drops off to the left. When you've crossed the gully at 1.7 miles at the triple white blaze, pause at the other side to search the shady nooks around the rocks. From April through July, you'll find a delicate lantern-shaped wildflower known as columbine. Use a magnifying glass to examine its deep red flower, which hangs down because the petals grow backward in tubular spurs. In her book *Wildflower Folklore,* Laura Martin reports that according to legend, "lions ate columbine in the spring to gain extra strength," and that columbine, which was used by ancient herbalists to treat a variety of ailments, "was found on the border of a handwritten manuscript that was dated in the late 15th century."

Leaving the boulders behind, you'll be treated to the wonderful aroma of pine as you enter deep woods at 1.8 miles. The trail soon swings left, descending steeply for a few yards. Turn left at the junction with a triple white blaze; mountain laurel is profuse along this

Hikers are treated to a panoramic view upon reaching the fire tower.

narrow section. In 0.25 mile, turn right at the two blazes marked with triple white dots, climbing gradually while surrounded by pines. If you've kept count of the boulders, at this point you'll have a few new ones to add to your total. At 2.5 miles, you'll be in an open area with more boulders and a fantastic view of the Clinton Reservoir. Keep going. The best is yet to come!

At the triple blaze at 2.9 miles, where the trail goes in two directions, go right, heading uphill. This leads to the fire tower. Before enjoying the 360-degree view, you might want to rest or have lunch at one of the picnic tables. Retrace your steps when ready to return.

12. Horse Pond Mountain

Type: Dayhike
Difficulty: Moderate for children
Distance: 4.3 miles, round trip
Elevation gain: 400 feet
Hikable: Year-round
Hours: Dawn to dusk
Information: Norvin Green State Forest
c/o Ringwood State Park,
1304 Sloatsburg Road,
Ringwood 07456; (973) 962-7031
Admission: Free

If you haven't been to this area for a while, you may be surprised at the lake that's suddenly appeared here. It's the new Monksville Reservoir, created in 1988 to serve northern New Jersey in times of drought. Because it fills the recreational needs of fishermen and boaters, it's part of the Monksville Recreation Area and Long Pond Ironworks State Park, the state's newest park. The land surrounding the 500-acre reservoir also offers excellent trails and great lookouts for hikers.

Sturdy hiking shoes are recommended because the trail leading to the top of Horse Pond Mountain is very rocky. There are two opportunities to appreciate the vastness of this 500-acre reservoir. The first is from the western shore, which is a close-up; the second, from an open area just below the summit, provides a panoramic view.

From Wanaque, drive north about 10 miles on NJ-511 (Ringwood Avenue), staying with this road as the name changes to Greenwood

Lake Turnpike. The parking area is on the left (south side), opposite East Shore Road, 0.5 mile after crossing Monksville Reservoir.

Walk south past an iron gate onto a wide gravel path marked with blue blazes. This is the northern terminus of the Hewitt-Butler Trail, an 18-mile-long mountain-hopper winding through the Skylands section of the state.

In a few yards, you'll walk through an extremely narrow pass that is an old railroad route. In earlier days, this area was blessed with thriving iron-mine and smelting industries, which were particularly

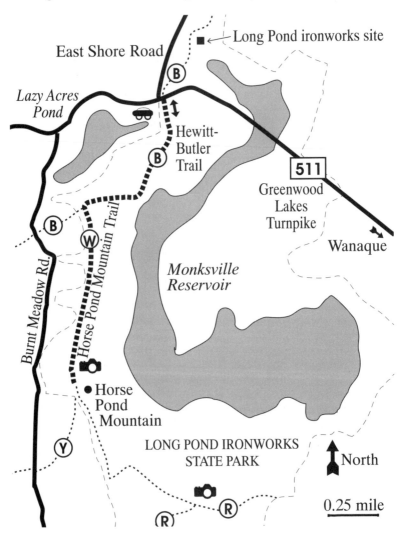

Winter is a great time to admire icicles hanging from the rocks along the trail.

important during the Revolutionary War for the manufacture of armaments. Steep cliffs flank both sides of the trail; in winter, icicles may hang down from the sheer boulders. The ice heated by the sun makes a soft, gurgling sound as it melts, reminiscent of a Japanese garden. Mostly level, the trail dips down and approaches the western shore of Monksville Reservoir. The opposite shore is so close that it makes the reservoir appear smaller than it really is. When you reach the top of the mountain, its true scale will be evident. Old tree trunks sitting in the water bear evidence of the recent flooding that resulted after the reservoir was filled with approximately 7 billion gallons of water.

The trail soon turns right into the woods and becomes narrow and rocky. As you climb past big boulders, you may catch the scent of sassafras. The soft pine needles underfoot in some places are a welcome alternative to the sharp rocks. There is a steep section over a huge rock wall at about 0.7 mile. Continue through a series of ups and downs, mostly ups, until you reach a junction with the white-blazed Horse Pond Mountain Trail at just under 1 mile.

Leave the Hewitt-Butler Trail and turn left, following the white blazes. A gradual ascent along the ridge for about 1 mile leads to an overlook with a marvelous view of the reservoir and surrounding woods.

This is an excellent place to have lunch and admire the scenery. The top of Horse Pond Mountain, about 0.2 mile farther south, awaits. While there is the satisfaction of having made it to the top, there unfortunately isn't any view from this spot.

At this point, you have a choice of three directions. One possibility (the one on which the mileage estimate is based) is to turn around and retrace your steps back to the start. If you'd like to experience more of the same type of scenery, you might want to continue another mile to the southern end of the Horse Pond Mountain Trail, where you'll be rewarded by another panorama. This will add 2 miles and some elevation gain to your round trip.

Regardless of which option you choose, consider visiting the remains of Long Pond Ironworks north of Greenwood Lake Turnpike. Watch for fast-moving vehicles while crossing this road. Find the blue-blazed Sterling Ridge Trail, which crosses into New York State and follows a woods road to the ironworks site in about 0.4 mile.

13. Stonetown Circular

Type: Dayhike
Difficulty: Difficult for children
Distance: 5 miles with car shuttle;
7 miles, round trip
Elevation gain: 600 feet
Hikable: Year-round
Hours: Dawn to dusk
Information: Not available
Admission: Free

Make certain you're in good shape before trying this hike. Several steep climbs are involved, as well as one long descent that's sure to leave your legs quivering from the exertion. However, the effort is worth it, because the ridges along the Stonetown Circular Trail offer spectacular views of the Wyanokie Mountains, Wanaque Reservoir, Montville Reservoir, and miles of forest. Hiking over odd-shaped outcrops—and the opportunity to pick blueberries during summer—adds to the enjoyment of being alone in lush woodland. Carry lots of water; on a hot day, you'll go through it quickly. Also, bring a magnifying glass or binoculars to examine the mushrooms on the forest floor. You might even spot a spider's web and, if you're lucky, may

Sitting on rock outcrops is a great way to appreciate the countryside and see the reservoirs atop Bear Mountain.

see an insect trapped in the web. Watch for a while and see how the web's slightest vibration sends a signal to the patient spider that dinner may be waiting.

Because of the length and difficulty of this hike, you may want to use a car shuttle. One vehicle can be left at the end of the trail so that it isn't necessary to complete the circuit on foot. For more exercise, you can hike the entire distance of 7 miles.

From Ringwood Avenue north of Midvale, take West Brook Road across the Wanaque Reservoir and make the first right turn onto Stonetown Road. It's a little less than 1 mile to the firehouse on the left. Leave one car in the parking lot there. Drive the other car(s) with all of the hikers north on Stonetown Road for about 2 miles and turn left on Lake Rickonda Road. Park at the end.

Walk back the way you drove in, along Lake Rickonda Road, with the lake on the left. Turn left at the T on Stonetown Road and then right onto White Road at 0.5 mile (there is a double red triangle blaze on a telephone pole), proceeding gradually uphill. Stately houses are to the left, shaded by a mix of maple, oak, and tulip trees.

At the double red blaze at the end of the road, at 0.9 mile, turn left onto a wide, rocky trail. In a short distance, look for a white arrow on a huge rock outcrop and head down into the gully. The only time the sun brightens this area is during fall and winter, after the leaves have fallen. Red blazes mark the trail, which makes a few turns in this section. Toads usually hang out among the decaying logs in this area. At the double blaze (1.2 miles) turn left and, as you cross a field of boulders a few yards ahead, watch your footing. After crossing the creek at 1.4 miles, head steeply uphill. A magnifying glass will reveal how closely the club moss that's scattered among the cracks in the rocks resembles miniature pine trees.

Blueberry bushes soon appear, and at about 1.7 miles the trail becomes narrow and level, but then quickly ascends again. In a few minutes you reach the overlook atop Board Mountain, where there's a fine view of Wanaque Reservoir and the surrounding woods. Follow the trail up and down along some outcrops. Where it dips again, at about 2.1 miles, a red cedar stands smack in the middle of the path. After a level section, the red blazes lead gradually upward again. The mountain laurel here is gorgeous, and in spring the blooms are especially grand. Another short, steep climb at 2.5 miles leads to a great view atop a wide, flat ridge on top of Bear Mountain, but during summer it may be obscured by foliage. Ahead is an unusual number of dead trees. Breathing in the aroma of fresh pine, you'll reach another vantage point facing the Wanaque Reservoir about 0.1 mile ahead. Be careful as you proceed downhill from here, as the grass hides some of the rocks and holes.

The blazes are far apart in this section, so don't go too far without making certain that you can still see the last one you passed. After a steep descent, the trail levels and continues over a series of boulders. At approximately 3 miles, you'll find two trees that seem to be hugging each other. On closer examination, it's apparent that the birch and tulip have grown and merged into one trunk system.

From here, there are several ups and downs, and at about 4 miles a steep climb will bring you to the crest of Windbeam Mountain with wonderful views to the west. Be very cautious when descending; the trail is very steep for several yards, but you can reach out to tree branches and trunks for support. After a dip, head uphill again. The next blaze is difficult to spot.

In a few yards, you'll reach another impressive westward overlook with water and forest below. From here, the going is pretty rough. Make sure to place your feet on solid rocks. A series of steps, made of logs and boulders, has been considerably placed to ease the way and prevent erosion, but the strain of holding back can be very tiring.

At the junction with Stonetown Road, a triple red blaze indicates the end of the trail. Turn right and continue about 0.3 mile to the firehouse.

14. Pine Swamp Trail

Type:	Dayhike or overnight camping
Difficulty:	Moderate for children
Distance:	5 miles, round trip
Elevation gain:	150 feet
Hikable:	Year-round
Hours:	Dawn to dusk
Information:	Morris County Parks Commission, 53 East Hanover Avenue, Morristown 07960; (973) 326-7600
Admission:	Free

A longtime resident of Morris County, Mahlon Dickerson (1770–1853) owned local iron mines, spoke several languages, and was a recognized botanist. Considering that he also served as state governor, U.S. senator, and secretary of the navy, it's no wonder that the largest

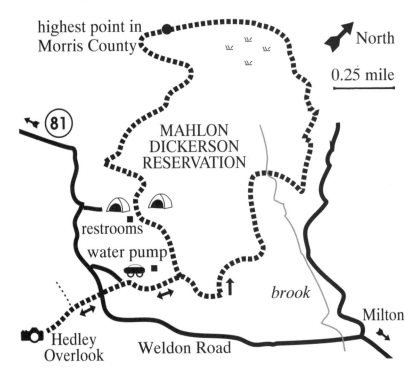

A rest break, especially on level, wide-open ground, is always appreciated.

park in Morris County—Mahlon Dickerson Reservation—was named in his honor.

The trails within these 1,500 wooded acres are situated along old logging roads, where you'll have ample opportunity to see impressive stands of spruce, azalea, and rhododendron. Although there aren't any views on the main part of this hike, a short detour at the end will bring you to an overlook with a terrific view of Lake Hopatcong, 9 miles in the distance. At one point, you'll also be standing at the highest elevation in Morris County. The park also has facilities for overnight tent and trailer camping.

From NJ-81 in Sparta take Weldon Road east toward Milton to Mahlon Dickerson Park. Park at the picnic area (second entrance on the left).

Walking north from the parking lot, you'll pass an old-fashioned water pump—perfect for filling a canteen and showing younger children what fetching water in the "good old days" was like. Continue ahead and turn right at 0.2 mile onto the Pine Swamp Trail. Not too many people can resist floating leaves downstream, so plan on a brief pause at the brook at 0.4 mile. Follow the double white blaze to the left, climbing gradually uphill past graceful tulip trees. If you're ready for another quick break, the 0.5 mile point is a good place to watch others practice rappelling on the huge boulders in this area.

From this point, there are many short ups and downs. After the right turn at 0.9 mile, the trail crosses a beautiful brook, a perfect place to listen to the music of the water as it swirls past a variety of odd-shaped rocks.

Watch for the white blazes as the trail makes several turns before entering the swamp for which it is named. Then, after a moderate climb, a sign announces the highest point in Morris County, which unfortunately does not feature a view.

The camping area, which appears a little over 1 mile ahead, is almost as popular with toads and garter snakes as it is with people! After entering the trailer section, continue past the restrooms and water fountain. From this spot, cut through the fence, forge ahead through an open field, following signs to the picnic area; this route returns you to the parking area. For an exceptional scenic view, find a trail heading south and carefully cross Weldon Road. Turn left at the sign for the "Hedley Overlook"; a short walk will bring you to the overlook with a long view that includes Lake Hopatcong. When you're ready, return the way you came back to the parking lot.

15. Assiniwikam Mountain

Type:	Dayhike
Difficulty:	Moderate for children
Distance:	3.3 miles, round trip
Elevation gain:	350 feet
Hikable:	Year-round
Hours:	Dawn to dusk
Information:	Borough Hall, Gould Avenue, North Caldwell 07006; (973) 228-6420
Admission:	Free; camping and fire permits available from Borough Hall

The tiny lake at the start of the trail covers only 5 acres, but its quiet beauty sets the mood for a pleasant, woodsy hike through part of Norvin Green State Forest.

Having lunch atop Wyanokie Ridge is a treat; in addition to the constant breeze, you'll have a terrific view of New York City's skyline.

A tree identification book is helpful, since you'll be passing hundreds of Mother Nature's natural air conditioners—trees. Among these are beeches, ironwoods, and oaks, and, like most trees, the slightest breeze activates their leaves, which, in turn, act as miniature fans.

From NJ-511 (Ringwood Avenue) just north of the town of Ringwood, go west on West Brook Road and turn left on Snake Den Road West at the sign for Camp Wyanokie. (If you come to Kitchell Lake, you've gone too far.) Park at Camp Wyanokie.

Keeping the lake to your right, walk past the cinder block picnic building along the Wyanokie Circular Trail, indicated by a red dot on a white background. Cross the dam at the beginning of the lake, follow the yellow and red blazes, and at the fork bear right, staying with the Mine Trail's yellow blaze. Walking uphill, you'll pass a natural rock

Wildflowers abound during spring and summer, and butterflies can be counted on to appear.

wall on the left. After a slight dip over large, flat boulders, the trail levels. Here, you'll find spherical galls on trees, evidence that insects have been depositing their larvae. The gall, formed as a result of that irritation, serves as both shelter and food supply for the parasite. If a tiny hole appears in the gall, the insects have already hatched and escaped. Break an old one open and you'll see the cozy sleeping quarters.

After a left turn, go slightly uphill past lush, old stands of mountain laurel. After about 0.7 mile, the trail reaches a well-marked junction with another trail that uses yellow blazes. Arrows and signs direct you to continue ahead on the Mine Trail (represented by an "M") or to turn toward "WC." No, WC doesn't mean there's a toilet in the woods; it stands for the Wyanokie Crest Trail.

Turn right and follow the WC Trail, a narrow, rocky path. A good place to observe chickadees is just ahead at a large, flat boulder with a trail blaze painted on it. Before starting out again, take a deep breath; the trail climbs steeply now, but there's a natural rock staircase to sink your feet into. Allow some extra time for the likelihood that your kids will play hide-and-seek in the many crevices. Another huge rock lies ahead, one shaded by overhead trees. Turkey vultures, frequently mistaken for eagles because of their 6-foot wing spans, usually circle this area looking for lunch. Thanks to eyes that act like binoculars, these birds of prey haven't any trouble spotting food from a mile away.

There are several panoramic views from the trail as it wanders around the top. Leaves may block part of the countryside during summer months, but the music they make as they sway in the breeze makes up for the lost view. Catbirds provide more music. After some brief ups and downs, you'll arrive at a flat ledge with Assiniwikam Mountain's most far-ranging and exciting view. Looking east, other peaks in the state forest are outlined by Wanaque Reservoir, and New York City's skyline is in the distance off to the right. If you're here when the sun is just right, New York's World Trade Center's twin towers look as though they're on fire.

After a few more ups and downs, the trail levels again and you'll come to another high spot. Here, too, trees block the view during summer. In July and August, blueberries grow profusely around the boulders and alongside the trail. At one point, an odd-shaped boulder to the right of the trail is supported by several smaller rocks. Soon you'll be atop another ridge and, after a gradual descent, you'll cross a trail marked in white. Continue on. Where the red blazes join with the yellow ones, turn right and follow the red-marked Wyanokie Circular Trail. Walking is a bit difficult in spots due to loose leaves and rocks. After descending, the trail follows an old dirt road to the starting point.

16. Osio Rock

Type:	Dayhike
Difficulty:	Moderate for children
Distance:	2.5 miles, round trip
Elevation gain:	400 feet
Hikable:	Year-round
Hours:	Dawn to dusk
Information:	Norvin Green State Forest,
	c/o Ringwood State Park,
	1304 Sloatsburg Road,
	Ringwood 07456; (973) 962-7031
Admission:	Free

Seeing the sunset from Osio Rock is memorable, but completing the hike in darkness can be tricky unless you're adventurous, there's a full moon, and you bring along flashlights and spare batteries for everyone. Even in full sunlight, it's sometimes rough hiking among the boulders, but the exceptional views throughout the hike repay the effort. Sturdy shoes are a must and a walking stick will come in handy.

Drive west on Glen Wild Road from Bloomingdale. After entering

Large boulders are encountered on the way to Osio Rock.

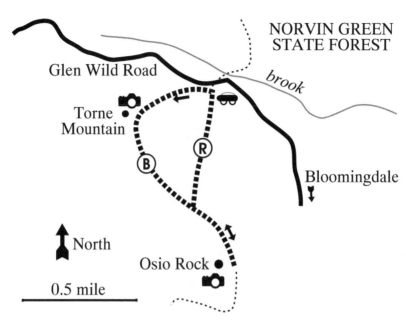

Norvin Green State Forest, park in the parking lot on the right side
of the road.

Cross the road and walk to your right for a short distance until
you see a tree marked with a blue blaze. Turn left, following the blue
markings that identify the Hewitt-Butler Trail. The brook you hear on
the right side of the road eventually empties into a pond. At 0.1 mile,
follow the blue blazes left, continuing uphill. When you pause for a
breather along this narrow, rocky trail, turn around; there's a fantastic
view of the unspoiled forest. At the first ridge, at approximately 0.5
mile, you'll be rewarded with an exceptional panorama stretching
endlessly into the distance. The few houses and tiny lakes are almost
hidden from view by dense forest and hills. In spring, you can see
colorful masses of rhododendron. Moss covers the trail in many spots,
making for slippery conditions. Watch your footing as you walk over
the boulders on this ridge.

Beautiful woods and lakes appear far below. The trail descends
gradually, and shortly you'll be on a flat boulder peering down at
mountain ridges to the south. At about 1 mile, you'll be descending
steeply on your hands and knees for a few yards before climbing again.
Continue straight ahead, still following the blue markings. Look for
the spot where red blazes appear on the left, as this marks the return
route. Continue uphill to the huge boulder atop another ridge at 1.4
miles. This is a good place to turn back if you're tired, but Osio Rock
is only a few minutes farther and well worth the extra effort. At this
high point, there are impressive views to the east and west.

When ready, retrace your steps. At about 2 miles, turn right onto the red-blazed trail, heading uphill for a short distance. The trail gradually descends and levels off; you'll be a few yards from the end of the trail when it drops again. Turn right at the highway and return to the parking area.

17. Wyanokie Mini-Circular

Type: Dayhike
Difficulty: Difficult for children
Distance: 3.7 miles, round trip
Elevation gain: 550 feet
Hikable: Year-round
Hours: Dawn to dusk
Information: Norvin Green State Forest,
c/o Ringwood Park, Box 1304,
Ringwood 07456; (973) 962-7031
Admission: Fee for parking

This hike through dense woods and the Wyanokies leads into Norvin Green State Forest, a hilly wilderness oasis. A couple of steep ascents and descents are involved, but the payoffs are the lovely views, the variety of trees, and the many inviting streams to rest beside.

Norvin Green is a popular family hiking location thanks to the efforts of the Green Mountain Club, which blazed these trails in the 1920s, and the care extended today by the Weis Ecology Center and the New York–New Jersey Trail Conference. Well-marked trails criss-cross the hills, reaching several peaks with extensive views of green forest. Plan on starting out early in the day so that you can take time to visit one of the local mines, leftovers from days long gone when the ironworks industry thrived in the area. These abandoned mines are often filled with water and can be dangerous; use caution to prevent injury. If in doubt, it's best to stay outside. To visit Roomy Mine, follow the alternate route at the beginning of the hike.

 From Wanaque, take Ringwood Avenue (NJ-511) north, turn left on West Brook Road, and left again at the sign for Snake Den Road. Park at the Weis Ecology Center (parking fee).

Walk east for about 0.1 mile and pick up the red-blazed Wyanokie Circular Trail, which passes between a few houses. All signs of civilization are soon left behind as the trail enters a grove of hemlocks.

The temperature can be several degrees cooler in these woods on hot summer days. Turn right at the beginning of the Mine Trail, marked by yellow blazes. The route leads over two small ridges, crosses Blue Mine Brook, turns left sharply, and soon crosses the brook again. The rocks in the water look picture-perfect and the sound of the water is pleasant as it falls down a steep chute. At a huge boulder, you'll cross the red-blazed trail before heading uphill to an open area with a pleasant panorama, a sample of what lies ahead.

Stay with the yellow markings as they turn toward the south. After some gentle meanderings, the trail dips down and twists to the right in front of the entrance to the Roomy Mine. This is one of the few abandoned mines in the area not filled with water. The opening leads into an antechamber open to the sky. Carry a flashlight so you can walk into the 60-foot-long tunnel. Water slowly drips from the rock ceiling and collects in tiny pools. Speak softly so as not to disturb any of the cave critters, such as the bats that hibernate here during winter months. When you are through exploring, continue on the Mine Trail; turn left where red and yellow blazes meet.

Blue Mine Brook, at 1.4 miles, is a great place to wet a bandana or sit and listen to the latest bird concert. From this point, you'll be walking close to another stream. At a wooden bridge erected by hardworking members of the New York–New Jersey Trail Conference, you may wish to turn around.

Otherwise, proceed straight, going up and down slight hills, until

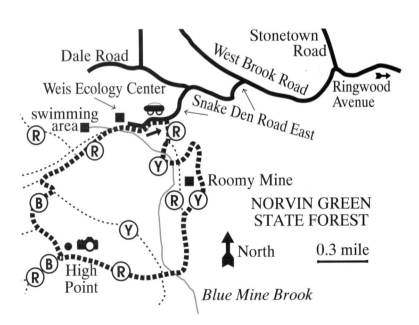

Norvin Green State Forest offers the hiker a variety of views and lovely trees.

a steep climb to the top of the ridge begins. The tall tulip trees in this area were prized by the Indians because their sturdy trunks were the perfect shape for canoes.

Follow the red trail to High Point and enjoy a 360-degree view, one of the best to be found in the region. To the east is Wanaque Reservoir, the largest in the state, with New York City's skyline in the distance. In every other direction, you can see lush green forests; and, if you're lucky, you will spot hawks soaring effortlessly on thermals.

In the spring, tiny parachute-shaped pink blossoms of mountain laurel, which abounds in this area, will compete for your attention. Blueberries are yours for the picking if you arrive during the summer, but make certain you know for sure what you're eating. To return, continue for about 0.1 mile, and turn right onto the blue-blazed Hewitt-Butler Trail. Bare rock in this area can be slippery from the morning dew or rain. The trail follows the top of the ridge past outstanding mountain laurel before descending along Blue Mine Brook and beneath a canopy of tulip trees. Turn right at the junction with the red-blazed Wyanokie Circular, and follow it back past a magnificent rock-framed swimming area to the starting point.

18. Tripod and Bear Rocks

Type:	Dayhike
Difficulty:	Moderate for children
Distance:	3.3 miles, round trip
Elevation gain:	300 feet
Hikable:	Year-round
Hours:	Dawn to dusk
Information:	Pyramid Mountain Visitor Center, 472 Boonton Avenue, Montville Township 07045; (973) 334-3130
Admission:	Free

This hike offers one pleasant surprise after another. Not only will you be passing through lush woods, but you'll have a fine view of New York City's skyline from the top of Pyramid Mountain. There's more icing on the cake: You'll see two excellent examples of glacial erratics—huge boulders believed to have been swept and deposited here by a glacial ice sheet around 12,000 years ago. Tripod Rock, balanced on tiny, ball-shaped rocks, is a 200-ton beauty, while Bear Rock casts a tremendous shadow upon the swampy area it monopolizes.

From I-287 North, take Exit 44 (Main Street in Boonton) to Boonton

A hiker admires Tripod Rock.

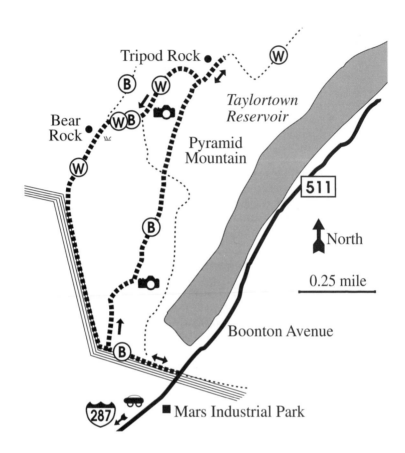

Avenue (County Road 511). Turn right here and continue north 3.3 miles to the Visitor Center parking lot on the left opposite Mars Court.

Sturdy shoes are recommended because the trail is rocky in many places. Follow signs to the blue-blazed trail and turn left onto it. Cross the footbridge at 0.1 mile, and take the short boardwalk over a brook. After a heavy rain, you might see a tiny waterfall in this area as you gradually ascend Pyramid Mountain. On the way up, you'll be surrounded by boulders and tall oaks. In about 0.25 mile, you'll begin to ascend a rock staircase thought to be laid by a construction crew many years ago. To the right are two large ball-shaped boulders that look as though they may fall with the first strong breeze.

After passing a power-line tower, and at approximately 0.4 mile, bear right at a blue-blazed post, staying with the blue trail and climbing steeply through a mixed forest of beeches, oaks, tulip trees, and red maples. A lovely pond soon comes into view, and as the trail levels a bit ahead, you'll be treated to a fantastic view of the World Trade

Center's twin towers. During autumn, the trees in this area resemble an artist's palette.

The trail heads downhill at 0.9 mile, and at 1.3 miles, where blue blazes lead to the left, continue straight ahead on a trail with white markings, which soon leads to Tripod Rock. This is a great spot to stop, rest, and try to figure out how the rock got here. You'll hear youngsters begging adults to hoist them onto the top of the rock and will see lots of fellow hikers creeping beneath it as well. When finished, backtrack down the white trail again, turning right at the double white blaze heading up and then downhill. Be careful in the fall, when leaves obscure rocks on the trail.

When the trail levels out, you'll be in a swampy area where sphagnum moss thrives. A short distance ahead, the woods take on a special cathedrallike feeling late in the afternoon. After crossing a bridge over a tiny brook, you'll come to Bear Rock at about 2 miles. Take your time to walk around and climb partway up. This is an excellent place to picnic and a good place to seek shelter should it suddenly start to rain. When ready, continue on the white trail, which leads through woods and then under a row of power lines. The giant towers supporting them are fascinating up close.

You walk through a clearing, with the woods on either side, and then there's a short climb that quickly levels out again. To the left are small boulders perched on huge granite walls. After heading downhill slightly at 2.9 miles, you'll see another tower. Stay right at the junction with the Butler Montville Trail and follow the blue markings east under power lines. In a short while, the trail leads down the rock steps you originally took and back to the parking lot.

Frogs

19. Turkey Mountain

Type: Dayhike
Difficulty: Difficult for children
Distance: 4 miles, round trip
Elevation gain: 340 feet
Hikable: Year-round
Hours: Dawn to dusk
Information: Pyramid Mountain Visitor Center,
472 Boonton Avenue,
Montville Township 07045;
(973) 334-3130
Admission: Free

Try this hike in spring, when the buds are bursting open, or on a hot summer's day for almost total shade while walking under a natural canopy of trees. Wear long pants so you won't get scratched by the occasional scrub brush or tickled by the tall grasses. Sturdy shoes are necessary for negotiating the endless boulders and slippery areas.

Before starting the hike, stop in at the Visitor Center; it is open Friday to Sunday. Pick up a map of the trails, check out the interesting exhibits, and ask for a calendar of events.

The land you'll be hiking on was used as a hunting, fishing, and gathering site for over ten thousand years by Native Americans. Many explorers followed, and evidence of their presence can be seen while walking past surveyors' stones and stone walls which marked homestead farms and woodlot boundaries.

From I-287's Exit 44, Main Street in Boonton, take Boonton Avenue (County Road 511) northbound for 3.3 miles. Park at the Pyramid Mountain Natural Historical Area lot, on the left.

From the parking lot, walk out the exit and cross the road. Take the yellow-blazed trail, a few feet to your right; it quickly passes an industrial park before meandering up and down through dense woods. Throughout the hike, you'll find boulders of all sizes and shapes. You'll also find lots of beech, recognizable by its smooth, shiny gray bark and large "toes" that seem to bury themselves in the earth.

At 0.6 mile, turn left onto the blue-blazed trail. After a rain, you might have to jump across a narrow stream. As you begin climbing gradually, watch for mitten-shaped sassafras as well as many oak trees. A bit farther ahead are good examples of glacial erratics.

Watch for the double blaze and turn right at about 1 mile. This side trail, marked by blue dots on a dark background, leads to a

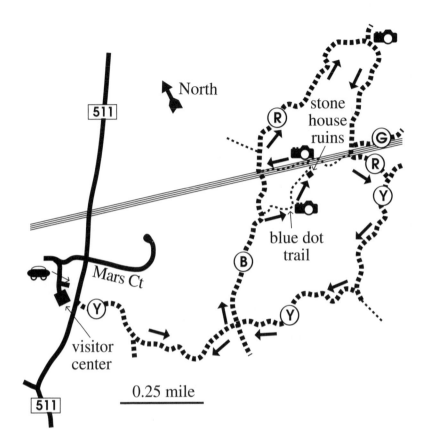

North

511

R

stone
house
ruins

G

R

Y

blue dot
trail

B

Mars Ct

Y

Y

visitor
center

0.25 mile

511

beautiful view of Lake Valhalla. When you're ready, head back to the blue-dot trail and continue to the remains of a stone house, built around 1910. A few feet ahead to the right is a terrific view of Manhattan's skyline. Turn left, at the powerline tower, onto the level, unmarked grassy trail, keeping the next tower in view. At the red trail marker (on a post), turn right into the woods and, while gradually heading uphill, examine the interesting tree trunks, but watch out for any protruding greenbriar.

Hold off having lunch or a snack; after bearing right at the fork and lifting your feet through high ferns and lots of boulders, a right turn will lead you to a huge boulder that's perfect for a rest break. The only time you can appreciate the distant view is during winter after the leaves have fallen, but in spring and summer months, you'll probably see a pair of doves that have claimed this area and keep circling for a handout. Identified by a long pointed tail, long neck, and small head, these birds emit a long, mournful cry that can be mistaken for an owl.

Check out the shrubs along the trail; you may come upon a praying mantis or other unusual insect.

As you descend down the red-blazed trail, Lake Valhalla comes into view straight ahead. Watch where you step; rocks are sometimes hidden by high grasses, and for about 0.1 mile the trail may be slippery. Be careful where it slants and falls away to the left.

The red and green trails meet at 2.8 miles. A short detour onto the green trail is recommended because it leads to a grove of ironwood trees and a pretty stream. Retrace your steps to the intersection, and follow the red-blazed trail through more shrub brush and tall grasses to the T. This is the end of the red trail, indicated by three red blazes. Turn right onto a yellow-blazed, fairly wide and flat trail almost devoid of rocks. In case you miss walking on the rocks, more turn up again as the road descends gradually through lush forest. After passing a narrow stream (at about 4 miles), take the right fork, still following the yellow markers, steeply uphill where the trail divides. Continue straight ahead when the blue-blazed trail crosses, pass the industrial center, cross the road to the visitor center, and return to the parking lot.

20. Ramapo Lake

Type:	Dayhike
Difficulty:	Moderate for children
Distance:	5.2 miles, round trip
Elevation gain:	220 feet
Hikable:	Year-round
Hours:	Dawn to dusk
Information:	Ramapo Mountain State Forest, c/o Ringwood State Park, 1304 Sloatsburg Road, Ringwood, NJ 07456
Admission:	Free

Why does a skunk start dancing? According to the National Wildlife Federation book *The Unhuggables,* it's how a skunk warns you to stay away before spraying musk, a smelly, oily liquid. Although you may very well meet one of these cute critters on the trail in this lovely 2,340-acre forest, you'll get several warnings before it sprays you. As a second warning, the skunk may violently shake its head from side to side. When it raises its hind end, you're in deep trouble.

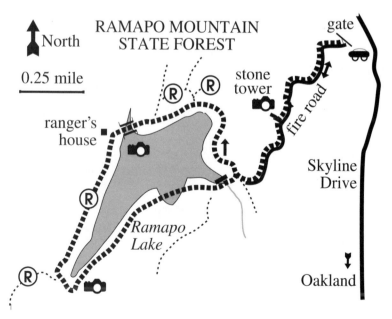

While hiking Ramapo Lake's perimeter, you may also see muskrat, which Dutch settlers referred to as the "rote," or rat. About the size of a cat, this furry brown mammal makes a roundish house of cattails and grasses in the water and can sometimes be seen prowling around the water's edge for turtles, fish, and various water plants.

For a short period, you'll be hiking the historic Cannonball Trail, a secret route through the Ramapo Mountains used during the Revolutionary War to transport cannonballs that had been cast in local furnaces.

From the junction of Skyline Drive and West Oakland Avenue (just west of Oakland), go north on Skyline Drive for 1.4 miles to the gravel parking lot on the left side of the road (opposite the Camp Tamarack sign).

Go past a gate and head southwest along a wide, flat fire road closed by a gate. Huge boulders, rich in iron ore and dating back millions of years, appear at 0.25 mile. Continue straight ahead when a side road comes in at 0.5 mile, and in a few minutes you'll reach a mysterious circular stone tower with antennas sticking out. Descending gradually, you'll soon see Ramapo Lake, which is reached at about 1.3 miles.

Turn right onto the level path that circles the lake. Colored blazes will occasionally be visible as other trails join in and then leave your path as you continue along the shore. You'll find huge stands of sassafras on the way to a tiny waterfall at 1.6 miles, an excellent spot to wet a bandana, fish a bit if you've brought a rod, and admire the scenery. Occasionally a frog will signal its presence by a "plunk, plunk" banjolike

Canada geese are frequent visitors to Ramapo Lake.

song, or a dragonfly—commonly called a "darning needle"—will plop down on a plant, resting between flights searching for a tasty gnat or fly. At the fork at 1.7 miles, bear left and continue to the bridge at about 2 miles, where you'll have an exceptional overall view of the lake. It isn't at all uncommon to find a rooster crossing the trail at the ranger's house a few feet ahead. Again, bear left along the lake when the road forks just ahead. You'll have another beautiful view of the lake at 3.4 miles, where the surrounding boulders make an excellent place to sit or climb. From here, there are slight ups and downs; stay with the gravel road as it continues the entire way around the lake. A bit past the dam (at about 4 miles), look for the fire road that leads back up to the parking lot. Try not to miss it; if you do, you may wind up circling the lake again.

21. Erskine Lookout

Type: Dayhike
Difficulty: Difficult for children
Distance: 7.7 miles, round trip
Elevation gain: 300 feet
Hikable: Year-round
Hours: Dawn to dusk
Information: Ramapo Mountain State Forest, c/o Ringwood State Park, 1304 Sloatsburg Road, Ringwood, NJ 07456
Admission: Free

On the Cannonball Trail, you'll be hiking along parts of historic Cannonball Road, the secret route used by the Continental Army for transporting munitions cast at Pompton Furnace. You'll also be atop the ridges of the Ramapo Mountains, where you'll stand beside a huge boulder, known as an erratic, that was glacially transported here thousands of years ago. The destination is an overlook with a terrific view of Lake Erskine and Wanaque Reservoir. An abundance of blueberries to chomp on during late summer is an added bonus. Long pants are in order for this hike; because the trail isn't used too often, you may be scratched by blueberry bushes or overhanging poison ivy.

From the junction of Skyline Drive and West Oakland Avenue just west of Oakland, go north on Skyline Drive for 1.4 miles to the gravel parking lot on the left side of the road (opposite the Camp Tamarack

Huffing and puffing—and even pushing—can't budge the glacial erratics found along the Cannonball Trail.

sign). (This is the same starting point as Hike 20, Ramapo Lake.)

Cross Skyline Drive (watch for oncoming traffic) and follow the yellow blazes of the Hoeferlin Trail (named to honor mapmaker and trailblazer William Hoeferlin). After a short climb, you'll see a sign pointing left to an Indian shelter. Archeologists have found hundreds of artifacts within the 6-by-12-foot stone formation, which was once used by hunters for shelter. Explore the cave now, or continue the steep climb among the boulders. In a few spots, you'll have to place your hands in crevices and grab onto trees to gain leverage. The trail soon levels, but the rest of the way—as you're surrounded by blueberry bushes and stands of mountain laurel, tall oaks, and beech trees—has gradual ups and downs. At about 0.5 mile, the trail turns; bear right at the double yellow blaze. When the Cannonball Trail (indicated by a white C on a red circle) joins with the yellow trail, it widens and is fairly free of rocks. Continue, turning left at the double red blaze at about 1 mile into the open. After walking a few feet along the road, turn right into the woods again, onto a rocky, narrow trail heading uphill and marked with red and yellow blazes. Turn left at the triple white blaze, at 1.5 miles, and follow the white markings a short distance to an overlook with a broad westward view of the Ramapo Hills and scattered lakes.

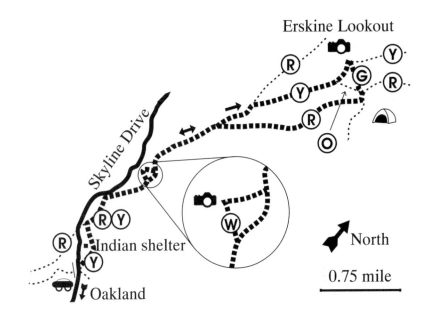

Erskine Lookout

North

0.75 mile

Relax here a while, or continue on, following the white blazes,
and turn left when you reach the Cannonball and Hoeferlin trails
again. After a little over 0.5 mile through deep woods and then over
boulders, double blazes indicate that the trails go their separate ways;
follow the yellow markings on a narrow path through a fairly rugged
but scenic area.

Stick with the Hoeferlin Trail when triple red blazes appear at
2.7 miles. After some easy walking over flat boulders, odd-shaped
boulders are underfoot for the next 0.25 mile. The large, round erratic
at 3.3 miles looks like a baseball suspended in air from a certain angle,
but it's actually supported by smaller rocks. Continue straight as orange
markings appear from the right at 3.6 miles; Erskine Lookout comes
in 0.2 mile, the high point of this hike. The view is extensive, with
Wanaque Reservoir serving as a backdrop for Erskine Lake, which was
named for Robert Erskine, a Scottish engineer brought here in 1771
to help solve problems Ringwood was having with its iron operations.
Erskine, who subsequently helped Ringwood to become one of the
most successful ironworks, was appointed general surveyor in 1777 by
George Washington, and also worked on the first clear maps of northern
New Jersey and southern New York.

To return, follow the arrow leading to the green trail and wind
your way downhill through the woods, past a scout camp's lean-tos.
When the Cannonball Trail reappears about 0.5 mile later, at the T,
turn right. Red maple, ash, hickory, and black birch shade the trail

on the way to the double red blaze, where you make a right turn (4.5 miles). The trail is wide here, but quite rocky as it gradually goes up and down hills. Take the right fork at the double red blaze, turn right heading uphill at another blaze, and as you begin descending you'll encounter a field of boulders. Be aware that leaves may hide holes between the rocks. Continue southwest, retracing your original outbound route as the Hoeferlin Trail joins in, being careful not to lose the trail in the vicinity of the first viewpoint.

22. Ramapo Reservation

Type: Dayhike
Difficulty: Moderate for children
Distance: 5 miles, round trip
Elevation gain: 600 feet
Hikable: Year-round
Hours: Dawn to half an hour after sunset
Information: Ramapo Valley County Reservation, 584 Valley Road, Mahwah 07430; (201) 825-1388
Admission: Free; permit, fee for camping

Ramapo Valley County Reservation boasts over 200 species of birds, but there's more here than the songs of warblers, mockingbirds, and woodpeckers. There are also the cool, shaded hillsides and ridges filled with majestic trees, flowering dogwood, mountain laurel, and pink azalea.

The hike, with many ups and downs, leads past numerous scenic spots including Scarlet Oak Pond, the Ramapo River, and the MacMillan Reservoir. Originally purchased from the Indians, this land had been the site of a farm, a grist- and sawmill, and a bronze foundry, before being purchased by the county with state and federal funding in 1972.

Sturdy shoes are best for negotiating this rocky terrain.

From Oakland take NJ-202 north about 5 miles. The entrance to the reservation is on the left. (If you come to Darlington Avenue, you've gone too far.)

From the parking lot, head into the woods and look for the silver trail (marked by a tin can cover on tree trunks). A plaque on a boulder commemorates where New York City hotel owner A. R. Darling built

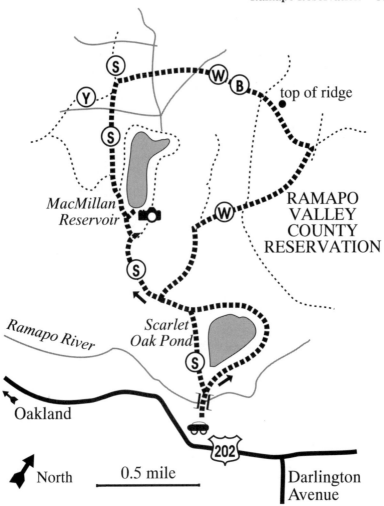

a mansion and operated a dairy farm in 1864. The land was purchased by the Bergen County Park Commission.

Continue over two bridges and turn right at Scarlet Oak Pond. With the pond on the left, the level, wide trail passes the Ramapo River to the right.

At 0.4 mile, bear left at the fork, following along the pond in sight of a meadow laden with wildflowers from early spring through fall. Queen Anne's lace, standing straight as a soldier, was named for its pretty blossoms that resemble a queen's headdress. According to legend, the deep purple floret in the center of this lacy flower is a drop of blood from a queen's finger.

You'll find Joe-Pye weed here, too; it's especially beautiful in late

Toads can frequently be found on the rocks skirting the trail.

August when it sports a cluster of tiny pinkish purple flowers. Supposedly named for an Indian medicine man who used the plant to cure typhoid fever, Joe-Pye weed was chewed by young Indian men who believed it would bring them good luck before a date.

Turn right at the junction with the silver trail and walk uphill following the tin markers. Shortly, you'll cross over two concrete bridges. After the second one, where boulders of every size and shape lie in the stream, swing left, continuing uphill at the double silver blaze. Bear right just after the third bridge at 1.3 miles for a sweeping view of MacMillan Reservoir. Return to the main trail and continue, climbing along the west side of the reservoir, where the water is nicely framed by surrounding forest. After passing the junction of the yellow and silver trails at 1.4 miles, the trail gradually descends and is rocky for another 0.5 mile.

Turn right into the woods at the triple white blaze and follow the white and blue blazes. Going down this section is a bit rough because of loose rocks, but it gets easier as it ascends again at approximately 2 miles. After a few ups and downs, turn sharply right, heading uphill to the blue and white blazes. The large, flat rocks up ahead at 3 miles make perfect seats for resting. Turn right near the top of the ridge. The trail goes through an open field, heading downhill once again on a wide, grassy trail with many wildflowers. This is a favorite nectar-gathering spot for bees. Turn right at 3.4 miles onto the white-blazed trail. The path is level for a while; at 3.9 miles, where you see double silver and white blazes, bear left heading downhill. There is a confusing mishmash of side trails in this area, many of them marked with tin-can blazes, so be careful to stay on course.

Continue on the rocky track, eventually joining the silver trail, turn left, and go past Scarlet Oak Pond and over the Ramapo River, back to the parking lot.

23. High Mountain

Type:	Dayhike
Difficulty:	Difficult for children
Distance:	5.1 miles, round trip
Elevation gain:	500 feet
Hikable:	Year-round
Hours:	Dawn to dusk
Information:	Not available
Admission:	Free

Early or late in the day, during any season, the climb to High Mountain is worth the effort for the panoramic view from the top. From the barren summit, you'll have an excellent view of New York City's skyline, the graceful lines of the George Washington Bridge, and the surrounding Preakness Mountain Range. At 879 feet, High

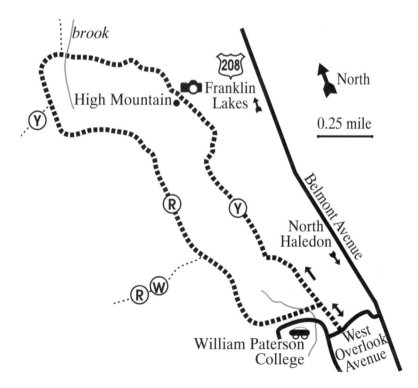

Mountain is aptly named, for this bald, rocky knob is the highest in the area.

Rarely will a furry creature venture too far from its warm burrow during winter months, but deer can be spotted here year-round foraging for a bit of tasty bark. Even in warmer weather, it's a good idea to wear a hat to protect against the constant wind. Sturdy shoes will also help guard against sore toes as you walk along the rocky trail.

From the junction of Belmont and Overlook avenues in North Haledon, head west on West Overlook Avenue, enter the grounds of William Paterson College, and turn right at the T. Park in lot No. 6, about 0.3 mile from the entrance and to the left. Walk back along the road and look to your left for three yellow dots on a rock behind a metal barrier just past the entrance. (Alternatively, from NJ-208 in Franklin Lakes, exit onto Ewing Avenue and head south. Turn left at the T on High Mountain Avenue, bear right on Belmont Avenue, and then turn right on West Overlook Avenue and proceed as above.)

Turn onto the yellow trail and head north. Proceeding slightly uphill, you'll have a view of North Haledon, just below on the right. Bear right, continuing on the yellow trail when the red blaze appears at about 0.1 mile, and head downhill for a few yards. After a short, gradual ascent, the rocky trail levels and widens, but gradually dips at 0.7 mile. The large boulders in this area are perfect for relaxing on while admiring the stands of beech, birch, and oak.

At just under 1 mile, ascend again. The trail eventually levels and dips before climbing once more at 1.5 miles. Thankfully, an abandoned truck on the right side is almost completely rusted and blends in with the fallen red oak leaves.

Climbing steeply, you'll leave all signs of civilization behind— except for some discards left by the uncaring few.

If it's winter, listen for its sounds: ice crunching beneath your feet and, occasionally, a tree limb falling under the weight of ice and snow. New York City's skyline appears to the right, just below the crest of High Mountain. The foliage begins to disappear and the trail widens as you continue uphill next to stands of sumac.

When you feel gusts of wind, you'll know you're just a few yards from the summit. The very top is completely open; spend some time walking around and absorbing the beauty of the surrounding mountains, the towns below, and the skyline. When ready, scout a bit for the next blaze, which can be found on a boulder. A bunch of trails converge at this spot, but with some searching you'll find yellow blazes leading down into the woods. Deer tracks are fairly common in this area. The descent soon becomes quite steep; watch where you place your feet because fallen leaves tend to cover up holes.

After a few ups and downs, you'll hear cascading water and, at 2.5 miles, will see a lovely brook a few yards ahead. You might not

Geology buffs will have a ball identifying the rocks found along the trail and the boulder walls.

want to look to the right at this point (you'll know why when you arrive). After you cross a wide trail, climb up the mountainside following the yellow blazes. It's steep, but short. There are many downed trees if you want to rest, as well as many trees to hold on to in slippery spots. At the top, turn left onto the wide, level trail that, for a few yards, is almost free of rocks. Just when you think there's free sailing ahead, the trail becomes rocky once more.

At the trail junction at 2.8 miles, continue straight ahead following red blazes as the yellow trail heads off to the right. This return route goes around High Mountain and is fairly level. The trail can be quite wet in places in spring or after winter melts, but it's wide, allowing easy detours around wet spots. After a grove of junipers at 3.6 miles, the trail descends and, 0.3 mile later, climbs gradually over large, bare rocks before leveling in a few yards. At the Y at 4 miles, stay left as a trail marked in red and white goes off to the right. A road is visible to the right at about 4.7 miles; just ahead, you'll cross a pretty brook. It's especially beautiful during winter months, when icicles cling to fallen logs and boulders. When you reach the yellow trail at 4.9 miles, turn right, and return to the start.

24. Palisades Boulder Field

Type: Dayhike
Difficulty: Difficult for children
Distance: 4.4 miles, round trip
Elevation gain: 530 feet
Hikable: Year-round
Hours: Dawn to dusk
Information: Palisades Interstate Park Commission, P.O. Box 155, Alpine 07620; (201) 768-1360
Admission: Free

This awesome hike begins from the highest point of the New Jersey Palisades and steeply descends 530 feet to the Hudson River. Part of the trail is an obstacle course through a sea of boulders, and part is a series of stone steps leading downward.

Wear sturdy hiking shoes because some of the huge rocks are smooth and slippery. Although this hike is strenuous in places, the views beneath volcanically formed vertical columns are exceptional. No doubt, Giovanni de Verrazano was impressed when he discovered the Palisades, which he referred to as a "fence of stakes." Heavy quarrying once threatened this area, but when Congress established the Palisades Interstate Park Commission, the natural beauty of these basaltic cliffs was preserved for all to enjoy. The New Jersey section, which dates back about 12,000 years to the Ice Age, has been named a National Historic Landmark and also a National Natural Landmark.

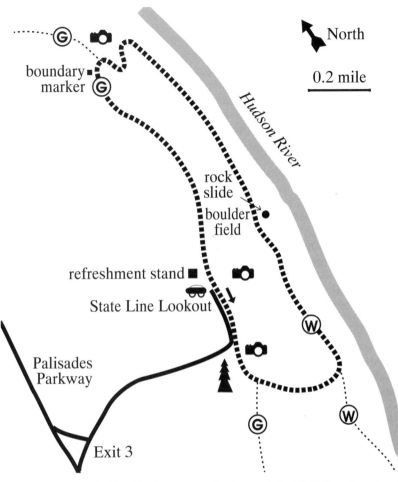

From the Palisades Interstate Parkway, take Exit 3 and park at
State Line Lookout.

Starting at the State Line Lookout refreshment building, walk
south along the entrance road you came in on. At a tree marked with
a green blaze and a sign warning that the "slopes are dangerous," turn
left into the woods. You'll immediately see one of the cliffs and, to
the left, an open area affording an exceptional view of the Palisades
and the Hudson River.

Use caution walking down the steep stone steps. Don't try to keep
count of them; you'll need all the concentration you can muster to
keep your balance and to admire the rocky surroundings. During the
winter, water running down the side of the cliff sometimes freezes

into icicles that glisten like diamonds. Bear left at the trail junction; be careful walking along the edge, which is unprotected and sometimes slippery. The steps just ahead will wind in and out along the edge of the cliff for about 0.5 mile until you're level with the water. At this point, turn left (north) along the trail marked with white blazes.

After about 0.25 mile of easy walking along the shoreline, you'll have a fine view of Indian Head peering down at you from the cliff. A short distance later, the trail leaves the shore and climbs steeply around the base of a large rock slide. Kids may have to use their hands and feet to climb over the larger boulders, but will love every minute of the challenge. When the trail levels off, you might want to stop to regain your breath, have a drink "on the rocks," look up at the nearly vertical cliff face, or check out the passing boats.

Continuing, you'll have a bird's-eye view of tulip trees and a rare view of their seed pods. Although the trail is nearly level, the climb over huge boulders seems endless at times. Pay attention to your footing, taking care not to get stuck in the deep cracks between boulders. You'll be happy you wore your hiking shoes as you clamber over smooth-faced rock surfaces.

Looking at the Hudson River from atop the Palisades

After a distance, the rocks give way to a dirt trail, and rocks and dirt alternate until the double white blaze is reached. Follow the trail as it again climbs steeply uphill by way of switchbacks. Caution: This section of trail follows along the cliff edge and it can be slippery after a rain. At the top, the aquamarine markings of the Long Path appear next to the triple-white-blazed trail. A short walk to the right, to the top of a small hill, reveals a spectacular view of the Hudson.

Turn left, climbing another series of steps, and look for rectangular fingers of rock pointing skyward. A New Jersey–New York Boundary Monument dating from 1882 is soon visible. From here, turn left going slightly uphill. After the trail levels, an old road that is now closed to traffic joins in and continues back to the parking area.

---

25. Lost Brook Preserve

Type:	Dayhike
Difficulty:	Easy for children
Distance:	4.25 miles, round trip
Elevation gain:	150 feet
Hikable:	Year-round
Hours:	Trail, dawn to dusk; parking lot closes at 5:00 P.M.; nature center, Mon.–Sat. 9:00 A.M.–5:00 P.M., Sun. 10:00 A.M.–5:00 P.M., closed holidays
Information:	Tenafly Nature Center, 313 Hudson Avenue, Tenafly 07670; (201) 568-6093
Admission:	Free

Before starting out on this hike, stop in at the Tenafly Nature Center to learn about the animals, birds, and insects that frequent the adjoining woods. A naturalist is usually available to answer questions, and, should you need additional information after the hike, you can return to browse through the library's collection of nature books.

The forest understory is aglow with wildflowers each spring, and there's an excellent possibility of spotting snakes during any season. Even though snakes don't have ears, they can sense vibrations you make on the ground and, almost faster than you can blink, they'll dart

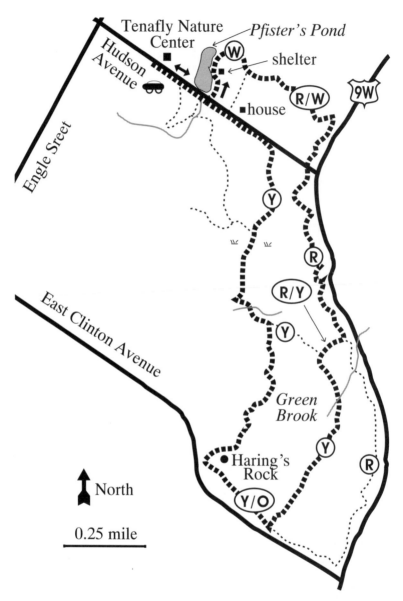

across the trail and disappear. On a sunny day, be sure to scan Pfister's Pond, a favorite basking spot of the northern water snake. Also check the underbrush for the tricolored milk snake, which was thought to milk cows because it was often found in barns. In reality, it was lying in wait for a tasty rodent. With a copy of Peterson's *Reptiles and*

Amphibians, you'll be able to identify many other snakes found in this area, including the garter and black racer.

From US 9W in Tenafly, take East Clinton Avenue west, turn right on Engle Street, and right again on Hudson Avenue. Park at the Tenafly Nature Center.

Waterproof, sturdy shoes are recommended to protect feet against rocky and swampy areas. From the parking lot, head southeast along a wide, level dirt road past many spring-flowering plants. The Indians made good use of many of these plants, including the arrowwood, whose strong shoots made ideal arrow shafts, and the five-leaved wild geranium, valued as a tonic. You'll also find bittersweet, which stays green all winter and was believed to cure bladder problems and kidney stones. After walking about 0.1 mile, you'll come to a tiny gem known as Pfister's Pond. Spend a few minutes observing the ducks. If you're here during summer, you'll see the spike-shaped flowers of the sweet pepperbush and the 1-inch flower clusters of the aquatic buttonbush.

Turn left at the far end of the pond onto a white-blazed trail where a boardwalk leads to an overlook shelter. This is an ideal vantage point from which to view the entire pond. Another boardwalk follows, meandering through a swampy area, with the pond to the left. After veering away from the pond, you'll begin a gradual climb into the woods. From this point, there are a few gradual ups and downs. Turn left at a double white triangle blaze at about 0.5 mile; from here, continue following the red-and-white markers of the Bischoff Trail. These soon give way to red blazes of the Little-Chism Trail. The trail meanders through woods thick with lovely sweet gum trees, which litter the trail with their 1-inch-round seed capsules. Trail blazes are far apart in some sections; to avoid losing the trail, be certain you know where the last one is before proceeding too far. In some places, blazes may appear on boulders rather than trees. There are swampy areas in this section of the preserve and, every so often, a beautiful stand of mountain laurel appears. There are also occasional small boulder fields. Keep an eye out for the tall, straight tulip trees. There is a majestic double-trunked specimen at about 1.5 miles. Leaves from the previous fall litter the ground in places, covering holes in the ground and making walking tricky.

Take a detour to the right at the sign for D Spur following the red-and-yellow blaze. The trail passes through a field of ferns. A few yards ahead is a beautiful beech, which clings stubbornly to its yellow leaves in the dead of winter. It's a delight to watch the leaves shimmer in the sun and shake with the slightest breeze.

Turn left at the junction with the yellow-blazed Allison Trail at 1.9 miles. Just ahead is Green Brook, a delightful spot to pause for a drink (food isn't allowed) or wait for passing deer. At about 2.5 miles, at a sign with a triple yellow and orange blaze, turn right onto

The shagbark hickory is only one of many interesting trees found here.

the Seely Trail. The boardwalk over the brook ahead will keep your feet dry, and at 2.7 miles you'll reach Haring's Rock, the largest boulder in this area. Turn right at the trail junction near this rock, onto the orange-blazed Haring Rock Trail. From here, the trail gradually descends. At the T, turn left onto the Allison Trail (yellow) again. This section of trail wanders past marshes and interesting (though small) rock formations. Make another left onto the dirt road at the triple yellow blaze marking the trail's end. You'll pass a large, private house on the right as you head back to the parking area.

26. Flat Rock Brook Park

Type: Dayhike
Difficulty: Easy for children
Distance: 1.25 miles, round trip
Elevation gain: 150 feet
Hikable: Year-round
Hours: Trails, dawn to dusk; Center for Environmental Study, daily 9:00 A.M.–5:00 P.M.
Information: Flat Rock Brook Center, 443 Van Nostrand Avenue, Englewood 07631; (201) 567-1265
Admission: Free

Working without pay, Englewood families scraped graffiti from an abandoned stone quarry and cut 3.5 miles of trails through land with 180-million-year-old volcanic bedrock formations, wetlands, ponds, a cascading stream, meadows, quarry cliffs, and one of the last remnants of the Palisades Forest. They also helped to design an impressive solar-heated nature building that houses a children's workshop and interesting exhibits. Why? To protect the city's open space while making the land available to everyone who enjoys the beauty of the natural world. They've succeeded. Visitors who hike the trails at Flat Rock Brook forget they're only a few miles from mid-Manhattan.

The surrounding woods are so dense that you're guaranteed shade on the hottest day, and during any season you're bound to catch a glimpse of a red fox or raccoon. Or a wildflower or toad. Walking the boardwalk a mere 0.1 mile affords a close-up look at jewelweed, which blooms from July through the first frost. Its bright yellow-orange flowers are thought to resemble jewels hanging on a necklace. Jewelweed's nickname is "touch-me-not" because if you touch it when the fruit is mature, seeds will shoot out. Boulders stand to the right of the brook you'll be passing.

From I-95 exit at Broad Avenue, Englewood and go north. Turn right at the traffic light on Van Nostrand Avenue and continue to the entrance of the park.

Start opposite the Flat Rock Brook Center building and gradually walk uphill on the red trail with the pond on your right. This immediately leads to woods where sweet gums and tulip trees tower overhead. The trail climbs to an overlook that provides a fabulous view to the west. Follow the trail as it veers left, and when the white trail appears, continue straight on the trail with red and white blazes. After the white blazes stop, the trail crosses into neighboring Allison Woods Park. A pond appears in about 0.5 mile.

According to local legend, a lady wanted her lover to build a bridge here. Although he wanted to, he never had enough spare time. But, after she died, he came back and built what became known as the "Phantom Bridge" because no one saw it under construction. Standing in the center of the bridge, you can watch the water as it falls over the dam.

Return over the bridge the way you came and turn right along the red trail. Shortly, you'll come to a brook with large, flat boulders— the reason for the park's name. Going down the steps at 0.6 mile, you'll hear the sound of water falling over the dam. This spot is so delightful that children may be reluctant to continue on the walk. In a few more yards, you'll come upon a small waterfall and into mushroom country. Walk down the steep staircase ahead, following the red blazes as you leave the water for a short while. Just when you're beginning to miss it, the water returns, and with it, hundreds of rocks and boulders.

A section of scenic Flat Rock Brook

At 0.9 mile, turn left, following the sign to the nature center. As you climb uphill, you'll see beautiful sweet gums in this damp area. Soon you'il be climbing steeply. At the double red blaze, bear right slightly. Not too many children can resist taking time out to climb on the boulders that appear a short distance ahead, but tell them to be careful because some are slippery. The trail levels out before climbing gradually again, and then the nature center building comes into view. At just under 1 mile, turn left, following the sign to the parking area.

27. Paulinskill Valley Trail

Type:	Dayhike
Difficulty:	Easy for children
Distance:	4 miles, round trip
Elevation gain:	Negligible
Hikable:	Year-round
Hours:	Dawn to dusk
Information:	Paulinskill Valley Trail Committee, P.O. Box 175, Andover 07821; (908) 684-4820
Admission:	Free

It isn't difficult to imagine another era while hiking the abandoned New York, Susquehanna, and Western Railroad's flat, narrow bed. Trains transporting coal, milk, and other goods played an important role in boosting New Jersey's economy. However, by 1962, trucking proved to be a more economical way to deliver merchandise, and

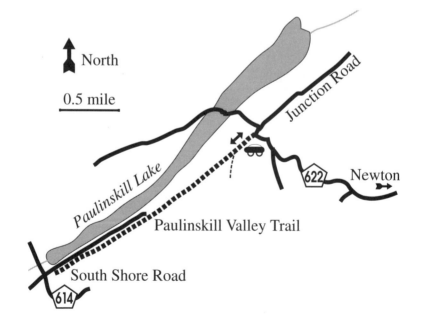

Colorful thistles can be found along the abandoned railroad bed.

a 26-mile-long section of track was removed. The City of Newark purchased the bed, planning to use it as a water pipeline for the proposed Tocks Island Dam.

When the project fell through, dozens of organizations began urging the state to acquire this property, known as the Paulinskill Valley Trail. Their efforts were successful, for today the right-of-way belongs to the State of New Jersey and hikers, joggers, and horseback riders have permanent access.

The trail goes through dense woods and fields in Warren and Sussex counties, following along the scenic Paulinskill River. Telegraph poles and occasional railroad ties remain on both sides of the trail, and there's a great variety of trees and wildflowers on this 2-mile-long section of the trail.

From Newton take NJ-622 (Clinton Street in Newton) west, following signs to Swartswood State Park. Park off the road on the left, opposite the beginning of Junction Road. If you cross the bridge over Paulinskill Lake, you've gone too far.

Walk southwest from the parking area into the woods, and bear right at the fork at 0.2 mile. The concrete abutment to the right supported a bridge that carried trains over NJ-622. A bit farther ahead, the trail dips between two ridges and, at 0.5 mile, when the land drops off to the right, you'll see a lovely forested hill on the left. Paulinskill Lake appears on the right at about 0.75 mile.

If you're here in summer, you'll feel cool while gazing down upon the water because a thick canopy of oak and maple shades the path. You may pass riders on horseback or hear water-skiers occasionally, but they won't be too distracting in these peaceful surroundings. At about 1 mile, the trail passes between huge slabs of rock. Spend a few minutes exploring; young trees have sprouted in the cracks of the rock, and you'll notice horizontal layers of slate. A few yards farther is another view of the lake and, shortly thereafter, a few houses and log cabins appear along the bank below. The end of the lake comes into view at just under 2 miles. A barricade and pile of slate at a high point overlooking NJ-614 mark the end of this section of the trail.

Return the way you came. Now that you've had time to admire the lake and foliage, you might want to identify some of the birds or search for old railroad spikes or railroad ties hidden in the brush along the side of the trail.

28. Dunnfield Creek Circular

Type:	Dayhike or overnight backpack
Difficulty:	Moderate for children
Distance:	3.4 miles, round trip
Elevation gain:	600 feet
Hikable:	Year-round; weekdays best
Hours:	Dawn to dusk
Information:	Park Headquarters, Delaware Water Gap National Recreation Area, Bushkill, PA 18324; (570) 588-2435
Admission:	Free

More than 2.5 million people are drawn to the Delaware Water Gap National Recreation Area each year. Most go directly to the Kittatinny Point visitor center, where they can enjoy a leisurely picnic or views of the scenic Delaware River. Hikers, however, come for the

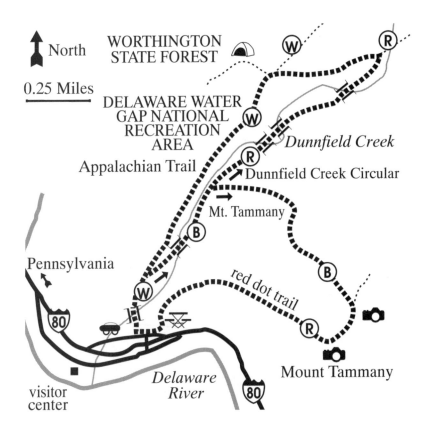

peace of the surrounding woodland trails on the Kittatinny Ridge and over a huge boulder dating back 450 million years.

On this circular hike, which includes a section of the famous Appalachian Trail, you're bound to see wildlife. You'll also see and hear Dunnfield Creek as it melodiously tumbles down on its way to the Delaware River. Each season offers a new delight. Spring ushers in new ferns; the fragrance of honeysuckle fills the air during summer, when the rhododendron put on a magnificient display; in fall, the leaves turn, casting a bright glow against a backdrop of tall, green hemlocks; and, in winter, a sheet of ice covers the stream's pools, while a blanket of snow decorates the rocks.

From I-80 West, exit after the 3-mile marker at the sign for the rest area, and park in the second parking lot (just past the rest area). From Pennsylvania, exit I-80 after crossing the Delaware River; pass the Kittatinny Point visitor center and turn left, crossing under the interstate. Turn left at the T and enter the parking lot.

Walk to the northern end of the parking lot and enter the woods

on the Appalachian Trail, indicated by double white blazes. Dunnfield Creek, on the left, with all sizes and shapes of boulders strewn along its bed, casts a special spell. The mating song of bullfrogs can be heard each spring and, at the wooden bridge just ahead, is the perfect place to pause and listen to the music of the creek as water makes its way past downed trees and boulders. Walk straight ahead and you'll see many trees crowding the edge of the creek. With their roots reaching into the water like giant toes, the trees suck up hundreds of gallons of water daily; ultimately, the water finds its way from the fine root hairs to the branches and leaves. There are also lots of tree roots spread across the trail, so watch your footing.

After a gradual climb, bear right at the fork. As you continue uphill, you'll come across mini-waterfalls here and there cascading through cracks in the boulders. After the trail junction sign for Worthington Forest, go slightly downhill onto the right fork at 0.3 mile, following the blue-blazed trail that soon narrows. If it's a hot day, you might want to cool off by dipping into the creek, now on the right.

Cross the wooden bridge and, if it's been raining heavily, you'll see more tiny waterfalls. Continue going uphill, following the blue blazes. At the fork, go left onto the red trail, which will soon take you past a swampy, level area, with the creek to the left and a hill to the right. Waterfalls appear one after the other now, and when you swing next to the creek again, you'll probably encounter lots of birds. The next bridge is at 0.7 mile; just beyond it is another.

In a few yards, you'll come to a large, downed tree—a perfect seat from which to observe birds flitting from limb to limb and bees gathering nectar from blooming shrubs. Head slightly uphill from here; the creek will be below you to the left. As you walk farther away from the creek, the trail levels out but becomes quite rocky. At 1 mile, tall tulip trees loom overhead; the fifth bridge is at 1.14 miles. Continue slightly uphill, and at the T at 1.4 miles, where the red trail swings to the right, take the left fork onto the Holly Springs Trail. Go uphill for a few yards on the wide, rocky path, continuing straight as it becomes grassy and passes through a lovely field of ferns. At 1.9 miles, the Appalachian Trail appears again opposite a sign for Backpack Site No. 1 on the south side of the trail. (If you plan to camp, there is no fee, but check in at the visitor center first.) Turn left here, going downhill gradually on an extremely rocky path. Look out for loose rocks. The trail changes into a level dirt path at 2.2 miles, and dips again in 0.25 mile before leveling. Dunnfield Creek comes into view once more to the left at 3 miles. Continue back to the first bridge and the parking lot.

The wooden bridge over Dunnfield Creek at the beginning of the trail

29. Mount Tammany

Type:	Dayhike
Difficulty:	Difficult for children
Distance:	4.3 miles, round trip
Elevation gain:	1,180 feet
Hikable:	Year-round
Hours:	Dawn to dusk
Information:	Park Headquarters, Delaware Water Gap National Recreation Area, Bushkill, PA 18324; (570) 588-2435
Admission:	Free

You'll huff and puff hiking up the steep, rocky trail to Mount Tammany's summit, but the reward is a spectacular view of the Delaware Water Gap, Mount Minsi, and surrounding farmland. Plan on frequent rest stops on the way up and be sure to carry ample water. During summer months, you might want to take a refreshing dip in Dunnfield Creek or simply watch the water as it cascades through large boulders and fallen trees on its journey to the Delaware River.

Mount Tammany, located within the 70,000-acre Delaware Water Gap National Recreation Area, is part of the wooded mountain ridge known as the Kittatinnys—from an Indian name meaning "Big Mountain." At the top, a perfect spot to admire the Delaware River as it cuts through the mountains, you'll also see turkey vultures and broad-winged hawks gliding on the wind currents.

According to geologists, when the flat-lying rocks below folded, erosion beveled them, but later uplift of the area caused the rivers and streams originally there to cut downward. As the land rose, the main stream probably maintained its old course, thereby separating the valley into bands of resistant and nonresistant rock. Water then eroded the softer materials while passing around the harder rock of emerging ridges. Eventually, the main stream formed a ridge and the notches or "water gaps" now visible.

 From I-80 West, exit after the 3-mile marker at the sign for the rest area and park in the second parking lot (just past the rest area). From Pennsylvania, exit I-80 just after crossing the Delaware River; pass the Delaware Water Gap visitor center and turn left, crossing under the interstate. Turn left at the T and enter the parking lot.

Walk for a few yards into the woods on the north side to the white

Hikers are rewarded after huffing and puffing along the steep trail by a spectacular view of the Delaware Water Gap and surroundings.

blazes that mark the Appalachian Trail. Follow this trail across a small bridge. The path gradually ascends, paralleling Dunnfield Creek. At 0.3 mile, at a sign and map for Worthington Forest, the trail divides; take the right fork, following the blue blazes. Cross a second bridge at 0.7 mile; after heavy rains, there are usually a couple of mini-waterfalls tumbling over the rocks on the left. The trail climbs for about 0.1 mile and then divides. Once again, take the right fork and continue to follow the blue blazes as they lead relentlessly upward. Although the trail is steep, the lush stands of oak, hickory, and tulip provide pleasant distractions, and during late spring, masses of mountain laurel bloom near the top of the ridge. The Delaware River pops into sight at the trail's highest point, but the best view is less than 5 minutes away. Turn right and follow the blue markers to an open area. A short walk onto the large boulders reveals a magnificent panorama containing the river and Mount Minsi on the Pennsylvania side. This spot, perhaps New Jersey's most scenic overlook, is perfect for eating lunch and watching canoeists paddling far below.

From here, continue right onto a trail marked with a red circle on a white background. This rocky trail passes a magnificent stand of mountain laurel before starting to descend gradually. After about 0.5 mile, the going becomes slow and difficult as the trail drops rapidly over a steep rock face. Use caution when you reach the steep section and be sure you have a good foothold when climbing down the rock. In this area, mountain ridges are visible in the distance and hemlocks tower overhead. You'll get another glimpse of the river before reaching the rest-area parking lot. Walk past the picnic tables at the west end and follow a dirt path that climbs over a small ridge leading, in less than 0.2 mile, to a second parking area and your vehicle.

Mountain laurel bursts into bloom each spring and stands out against the snow in winter.

30. Van Campen Glen

Type: Dayhike
Difficulty: Moderate for children
Distance: 2 miles, round trip
Elevation gain: 200 feet
Hikable: Year-round
Hours: Dawn to dusk
Information: Park Headquarters, Delaware
Water Gap National Recreation
Area, Bushkill, PA 18324;
(570) 588-2435
Admission: Free

Surprisingly few hikers try this short but challenging trail. Those who do have a wonderful adventure, for they can enjoy the phenomenal beauty encountered every step of the way. Despite a couple of hair-raising short climbs from ledges with sharp dropoffs, the sight of Van Campen Brook's many exquisite cascades is well worth the effort. It's several degrees cooler within the glen on hot summer days, and during fall the trees are a patchwork of color against the gray boulders. Have lunch or a snack in front of the upper waterfall—a musical as well as visual treat.

From the Kittatinny Point visitor center, take the Old Mine Road north for 10 miles and turn right at the sign for Van Campen Glen and proceed to the parking.

Sturdy shoes are essential for negotiating the damp, moss-covered rocks and logs. Walk to the water's edge, turning left along a narrow,

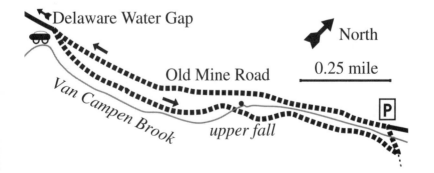

rocky, unmarked trail beside Van Campen Brook. Carefully negotiate the array of odd-shaped boulders and bothersome tree roots. As you make your way up and down, the brook is never far away, and if you stop to catch your breath, you'll hear the melody of the water as it flows on its way to the Delaware River.

An enormous boulder stands smack in the middle of the path at 0.2 mile—a perfect spot for soaking in the beauty of the tumbling cascades before you and for checking out the ferns that thrive in these moist woods. At this point, climb gradually away from the brook. The rocks are extremely slippery here, and as you grab roots and tree trunks for support, you'll probably want to rename this trail "Hug A Tree." The trail levels in a few yards, with a grand view of a waterfall below and to the right. While passing by, glance behind you to see where a tree has sprouted up from a crack in a large boulder. Climbing gradually again, the trail widens. At about 0.25 mile, water cascades over wide rock ledges. The trail rises steeply, levels, and gradually descends, reaching the brook once more.

You'll know when you've reached the upper fall, for the falling water has a deafening roar. Just before this spot, at 0.6 mile, there's a safe place to cross over the brook. The rocks are slippery, but if you take your time, your feet won't get wet. Once across, listen to the birds, admire the tall hemlocks, or perhaps cast for native trout. If you want to fish, you have to use artificial bait and have the proper permit. When you've filled yourself with the marvelous sight of the tumbling water, head toward the falls. Stay to the right side of the falls and climb over the big rock ledges next to it. An added bonus to these beauties are the two beyond it! At the top, you'll reach a flat area where water tumbles down through an impressive gorge. Keeping the water to your left, walk straight; shortly, you'll come to an impressive spot where the flowing water has carved out a narrow path.

Continuing, you'll need some tricky maneuvers to get over tree roots and rocks as the trail narrows. At about 0.8 mile, gradually make your way up the hillside to the level area and continue straight ahead to a rock boundary wall. Proceed through the wide opening, heading straight on this level path. The brook is now far below to the left. At the T at 1 mile, stop and consider your options. One is to turn around and return by the trail along the brook. The other is to turn left, crossing the narrow bridge over the brook.

When you reach Old Mine Road, turn left. Few cars use this road, but exercise caution on the way back to the turnoff and parking lot. Built by the Dutch in the mid-seventeenth century to transport ore from the Pahaquarry copper mine to Esopus (now Kingston) on the Hudson River, Old Mine Road was the first road built in the United States. The glen sits to the left far below the road. To return to the parking area, turn left a few yards after the downhill section begins.

Children atop the ridge overlooking the upper falls as it cascades into Van Campen Brook.

31. Three Mountain Ponds

Type:	Dayhike or overnight backpack
Difficulty:	Moderate for children
Distance:	5 miles, round trip
Elevation gain:	350 feet
Hikable:	Year-round
Hours:	Dawn to dusk
Information:	Kittatinny Point visitor center, Kittatinny Point, Columbia 07832; (908) 496-4458
Admission:	Free

What you'll find on this hike is great diversity. Each body of water is unique, and along the rim of each of these fascinating habitats—Long Pine Pond, Crater Lake, and Hemlock Pond—lies another world teeming with life. Salamanders, frogs, insects, and aquatic plants are only a few of the delights waiting to be discovered.

Pack a magnifying glass and look carefully when arriving at each pond. You may find snails clinging to the rushes and reeds. Or at Hemlock Pond, surrounded by a canopy of majestic hemlocks, you may catch sight of a beaver at work. There may even be a few deer nearby.

Most of the hike follows the Appalachian Trail. Sturdy shoes will help protect against the many rocks encountered on the narrow path.

From the town of Flatbrookville, near the junction of Warren and Sussex counties and the Delaware River, take the Old Mine Road

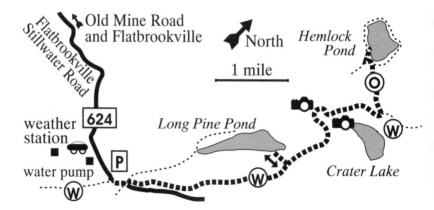

south for about 0.6 mile and turn left on NJ-624, the Flatbrookville Stillwater Road. The parking area is at the top of a hill in approximately 3 miles. An experimental weather station is set up in front of the parking lot, and a hand water pump (perfect for warming up muscles filling canteens) can be found off to the right.

Walk a short distance to the parking lot on the left side of the road and look for a narrow trail marked by white blazes that leads north into the woods.

The first half of this hike is along a fairly level stretch of the Appalachian Trail, much of it beneath a canopy of oak, beech, birch, and hemlocks, with lovely stands of mountain laurel scattered here and there. At about 1 mile, the trail descends steeply, requiring a bit of sitting and sliding. Grab onto tree roots wherever possible because the boulders can be very slippery after a rain or when covered by leaves in the fall.

Long Pine Pond soon comes into view on the left. At the double blaze at about 1.2 miles, detour a few yards to the edge of the pond. Fallen logs at the water's edge make an ideal spot to sit and enjoy the view, or to examine the lush carpet of sphagnum moss. Once back on the main trail, turn left and continue heading gradually downhill. After another 0.3 mile, there is a steep section over large rocks. When you reach the broad rock ledge at the top, look for Crater Lake on the right.

Old logging roads crisscross the trail in a few yards. There's a wonderful view of the surrounding ridges where the trail levels at the top of this ledge. In another 0.1 mile, where boulders are piled up, turn right for another fabulous view of Crater Lake. From here, you can climb down to the rim or continue on the main trail. If you're staying on the main trail, proceed slightly downhill as the trail widens, until it levels at 1.8 miles and another nice view of Crater Lake appears. An ideal overnight camping spot is 0.6 mile north.

Continue uphill, and just after a left turn on the trail, turn left at the Hemlock Pond Trail post (2.1 miles) and follow orange blazes, which are sparse in some places. During fall, the abundant oak and sassafras turn bright orange, and if you come in spring, the mountain laurel's pink flowers are in bloom.

Hemlock Pond magically appears in the distance at 2.2 miles, and is a hint of the reward to come. To reach it, follow the narrow, rocky trail as it meanders steeply downhill, goes up and down for a bit, and finally levels out on a wide trail. (Pay attention to the path you've followed, as several trails converge in this area.) Head for the pond when it comes into view again. Logs at the water's edge make a great place to have a snack or a moment of quiet reflection.

Return by the same route. On the way back, look for 3- to 4-foot-high tree trunks bearing the telltale toothmarks of beavers at work.

32. Jenny Jump

Type:	Dayhike or overnight camping
Difficulty:	Easy for children
Distance:	3 miles, round trip
Elevation gain:	280 feet
Hikable:	Year-round
Hours:	Dawn to dusk
Information:	Jenny Jump State Forest, Box 150, Hope 07844; (908) 459-4366
Admission:	Free; fee for camping

Legend has it that a girl named Jenny was so engrossed picking berries at the crest of the mountain ridge that she didn't hear Indians with raised tomahawks creeping toward her. Her father, standing below, saw what was happening and yelled, "Jump, Jenny, jump!" She did—and, unfortunately, was killed by the fall. At least that's what Swedish missionary Sven Roseen wrote in his diary in 1747, explaining how Jenny Jump Mountain was named. The Minsi tribe is long gone from the area, although it's doubtful that the Indians ever menaced Jenny at all.

A hiker admires a glacial erratic found along the Summit Trail at Jenny Jump State Park.

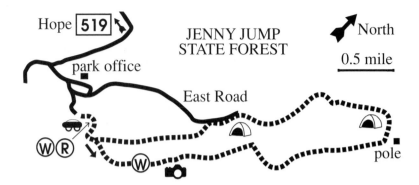

Situated about 12 miles southeast of the Delaware Water Gap, 1,090-foot Jenny Jump boasts excellent vistas of the Kittatinny Mountain Ridge, with sweeping expanses of farmland below. If you'd like to stay overnight, there are two group sites, six shelters, and sixteen campsites suitable for tents or trailers.

From NJ-80, take the Hope exit and drive south on NJ-521. In the center of Hope, turn left on NJ-519 north, and follow signs to Jenny Jump State Forest.

Stop at the park office for a map before driving to the first parking lot. Head uphill from the trail sign on the Swamp and Summit trails. At the double white blaze, turn right onto a wide, grassy trail, gradually continuing uphill to a narrow trail marked by red and white blazes. After bearing right at the fork, you'll find yourself beneath a canopy of hemlocks surrounded by huge boulders. The Kittatinny Mountain Ridge then comes into view, and where the trail veers left at the double blaze at 0.4 mile, head straight toward the single white blaze. Lush green farmland is below and to the right.

At 0.5 mile, where a double blaze indicates the Swamp Trail heading downhill, proceed straight ahead, going uphill along the Summit Trail. A rest is always welcome after a climb, and you'll have your pick of natural rock seats. When you've recovered, continue on to an open area along a ridge where the views get even better. The trail becomes extremely rocky at this point, with several easy ups and downs. Soon you'll descend again, and then start a long climb at 1 mile for about 0.25 mile. The rest of the hike is a piece of cake.

Turn left at the pointed pole at 1.7 miles. When you reach Group Campsite B, swing left again onto a dirt track that goes through the campground. Campsites are large and roomy, especially No. 20, which has a fabulous view (but the outhouses resemble upright coffins!). You can see one of the largest rocks in the park here, a rock left over from the Ice Age.

Continue past campsite No. 11 and turn left onto a dirt trail. In a few yards, you'll come to a sign for the Swamp Trail; turn right, passing through a lovely group of evergreens. At the double white blaze, bear right and continue to the parking lot.

33. Deer Park Lake

Type: Dayhike
Difficulty: Easy for children
Distance: 2.5 miles, round trip
Elevation gain: 140 feet
Hikable: Year-round; spring and fall are best
Hours: Dawn to dusk
Information: Allamuchy Mountain State Park, Stephens Section, Hackettstown 07840; (908) 852-3790
Admission: Free

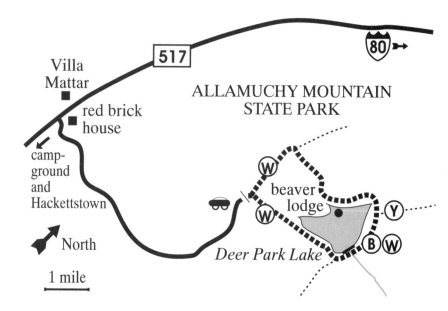

Trees provide a cool canopy on the hottest summer's day.

When you visit the north shore of Deer Park Lake, you may not see the broad-tailed beaver, the largest rodent in North America, but you will see its cone-shaped house and dozens of gnawed tree stumps. You'll also enjoy circling this charming lake, which sits in the serene wilderness of Allamuchy Mountain State Park.

Drive south on NJ-517 from Exit 19 on I-80 (toward Hackettstown), and make the first left turn at a post next to a brick house after passing Villa Mattar. Then proceed 2.3 miles to parking lot 2 at the end of the dirt road.

Cross under the gate at the end of the road and stay right on a level, wide trail marked with a white blaze. Here, ferns dominate beneath a canopy of beech, tulips, and oaks. The pond comes into view after 0.75 mile, and during summer or fall you'll be rewarded by the sight of water lilies floating in the clear, blue water. Proceed along the bank, turn left, and cross the concrete dam on the eastern shore toward the green oasis of evergreens, red maples, and sassafras. This is an excellent area for lunch or for children to skip pebbles across the water. A large fallen tree makes the perfect bench from which to view resident ducks and Canada geese.

From here, the blue-and-white-blazed trail climbs gradually. The open field 0.25 mile ahead is filled with colorful wildflowers in spring, summer, and fall; farther on, to the left, are mounds of black rock.

After a yellow-blazed trail comes in on the right, follow the trail as it hugs the north shore. Watch for signs of beaver activity. Children delight in discovering the beaver lodge at about 1.7 miles and examining the rodents' toothmarks on the remaining stumps. Walking on from this point, the pond disappears from sight and the trail enters another wooded area where the dominant tree is the red cedar. This is the highest point on the trail. Turn left at the T, heading downhill on the white-blazed trail. Continue straight ahead until you reach the gate you originally crossed under.

Note: Camping for trailers and tents is available at the Stephens Section of the park, located 2 miles north of Hackettstown on Willow Grove–Waterloo Road.

---

34. Pequest

Type:	Dayhike
Difficulty:	Easy for children
Distance:	1.7 miles, round trip
Elevation gain:	Negligible
Hikable:	Year-round
Hours:	Education Center, Fri., Sat., and Sun. except holidays, 10:00 A.M.–4:00 P.M.; trail, daily, dawn to dusk
Information:	Pequest Trout Hatchery and Natural Resource Education Center, 605 Pequest Road, Oxford 07863; (908) 637-4125
Admission:	Free

This hike is a golden opportunity for teaching children about natural resources, and for them to learn that corn is grown not in a can, but in row after row of open fields. You'll be hiking next to cornstalks over 6 feet tall. Resist the temptation to pick an ear; not only is it is illegal to pick or destroy vegetation, but this corn is only good for cattle. Upon close examination, you'll see that corn, a member of the grass family, has both male and female flowers on the same plant. According to Jorie Hunken in *Botany for All Ages,* the male flowers are "the large tassles of stamens at the top of the plant," and the female flowers are lower down on the stalk and appear to be dense clusters of strands of corn silk. Come during spring, summer, or fall, when the pastures are ablaze with colorful wildflowers and butterflies. Winter is fine, too, and is the perfect time for examining bark to identify trees in these serene woods where lichens thrive on fallen logs and rocks.

Allow plenty of time so that after the hike you can visit the Pequest Trout Hatchery and Natural Resource Education Center, where approximately 600,000 brown, rainbow, and brook trout are raised annually as stock for the state's waterways. After watching a short video describing the trout production process, take the self-guided tour. It leads to the nursery building and an observation deck overlooking concrete raceways where trout are kept until they're large enough to be released. Inside the center, try your skill at the "hands-on" exhibits. Bring along a fishing rod; the beautiful Pequest River is only a few steps away from the hatchery. Remember, though, that in the special Trout Conservation stretch between late May and early October only artificial lures and flies may be used, and that a fishing license and trout stamp are necessary for those over fourteen years of age, except during the annual "Free Fishing Days" in June.

From the junction with NJ-31 take NJ-46 east and follow signs to Pequest Trout Hatchery. Go through the main parking area and turn right on Pequest Road. Turn left on the gravel drive and park in the small space next to the kiln.

Until the 1930s, the kiln was used to burn chunks of limestone to produce a powdery lime for the farmers in the area. By spreading it over their land, they could temporarily restore the fertility of the soil by balancing the pH factor. Lime is still used by farmers today

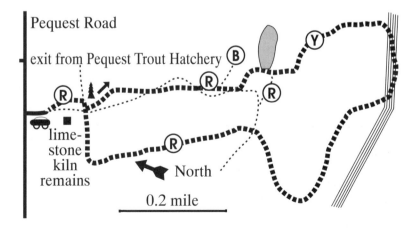

to reduce the acidity of their soil, but this type of kiln is no longer in use. To your left is the first of many cornfields encountered along this hike.

Walk slightly uphill for a few yards, following the red blazes. This narrow trail, surrounded by scrub brush, levels in a few feet before widening to a grassy path. Turn right at the T and look for Pequest's famous "honeybee" tree, a great black walnut. You may hear the honeybees buzzing as they busily transfer pollen they've collected from field plants into a hive in the tree's fork. The honeybee is New Jersey's state insect because of its importance in pollinating crops in the Garden State.

Continue past the tree, and make a quick left. The trail is wider now, flanked on both sides by a variety of trees and a low wall made of rocks that farmers have cleared from the surrounding land. The rusty patches seen on some of the stones show they contain iron. At this point, the trail ascends slightly. Soon after you're in the open. From here, you'll be darting in and out of the woods for a while. Views of rolling hills appear now in the distance, with cornstalks surrounding you in the summer months. At the junction with the blue trail on the left at 0.3 mile, continue straight on the red trail. Soon, it bears left, with an open field to the right and low shrubs to the left. A small manmade pond that attracts a tremendous amount of wildlife is at 0.4 mile. If you haven't spotted any of the local residents—deer, chipmunks, and groundhogs—check the tracks and droppings at the edge of the pond for signs of them. And look for the dragonflies that often hover over the pond like tiny helicopters.

As the red trail veers to the right just past the pond, continue straight to the yellow trail. Dozens of cattails stand in the marshy area to the right, as the trail, grassy now, continues with lots of mini ups and downs. The open field to the right is a favorite hangout for butterflies and honeybees. You'll soon enter woods, and as you climb up the rocky, narrow trail, watch for the lush ferns that grow in this low-light area.

You'll be in the open again once you reach a field and climb over a low rock wall on your way toward the power lines, where a nice view of the countryside awaits. Bear right under the power lines at about 0.75 mile. To the west, straight ahead, are pretty vistas; as you descend, farms appear in the distance. The trail parallels the power lines for a short distance, with woods on the right. Exercise care; this section of the trail is dirt with loose rock.

Cedars, the first trees to take over when open fields begin filling in, are to the right. When the trail levels at just over 1 mile, take a right turn, following the yellow trail back into the woods along the wide, flat, and grassy trail. Woodchucks may run across the trail when they hear you approach. Wildflowers also abound in this section.

The author examines the corn found in one of the many corn fields passed along the trail.

When you reach the red and yellow trail junction at 1.25 miles, proceed straight, to the red trail; 0.25 mile later, the open field affords a good mountain vista as the trail bears right. Turn left at the red arrow, where the trail is flanked by low rock walls. When you pass the honeybee tree, turn right and make a quick left, which will take you back to the parking area.

35. Merrill Creek

Type:	Dayhike
Difficulty:	Moderate for children
Distance:	3.5 miles, round trip
Elevation gain:	100 feet
Hikable:	Year-round
Hours:	Trails, dawn to dusk; visitor center, daily except holidays, 9:00 A.M.–5:00 P.M.
Information:	Merrill Creek Reservoir, 34 Merrill Creek Road, Washington 07882; (908) 454-1213
Admission:	Free

Swimming isn't allowed in the Merrill Creek Reservoir, but hikers "soak in" every ounce of the 650-acre body of water anyway. The water presents an exciting, yet calming effect. While hiking, you'll also be surrounded by more than 2,000 acres of forest and fields. The birding is excellent because migratory birds favor this area, and an observation blind is located in a protected cove along one of the trails.

Plan on stopping in at the visitor center before the hike. You'll learn how the reservoir was situated atop Scott Mountain, and how water is channeled into it and released from it. The water is used by seven electric utility companies in their generating facilities located along the river. After the hike, consider fishing; the water is stocked with trout, large- and smallmouth bass, and a variety of game fish. (A license is necessary.) Or, if you have energy to spare, hike the 5-mile-long perimeter of the reservoir; it has one section that involves a steep climb.

 From Phillipsburg, take NJ-57 east. In about 5 miles, turn left on Montana Road and make two left turns, onto Richline and then Montana Road (again). Follow signs to the Merrill Creek Reservoir Visitor Center.

According to naturalist Jane Bullis, "water to fill the reservoir is pumped from the Delaware River during times when the river flow is high." The water is carried underground through a 3.5-mile-long pipeline. Conversely, when the river is low, water can be released from the reservoir through that pipe.

After admiring the exquisite view of the reservoir and surrounding woods from outside (or inside) the visitor center, head for the gravel path on the side of the building that leads into the woods. It soon becomes rocky and narrow. At the fork with red and blue blazes, bear left onto the blue-blazed Shoreline Trail, which follows the perimeter of the reservoir. While gradually descending toward the reservoir, you'll be walking through dense woods of oak, tulip, and sassafras. The reservoir first appears to the left when the trail levels out in 0.25 mile. Continue to the water's edge, where you can appreciate the vastness of this manmade water basin.

When ready, walk slightly uphill away from the water. Soon the reservoir comes into view again where the trail levels. Proceed along the bank past a spruce grove at about 0.5 mile. As the reservoir disappears from view, you'll cross two boardwalks situated over a bog at 0.7 mile. Foundations of former farm buildings owned by the Cather family are in evidence, as are the rock boundary walls.

As you near a fork where the blue and red trails merge, bear left, continuing on the blue-blazed trail. At this point, look for the remains of a lime kiln. Farmers would transport limestone from deep in the valley to the top of the mountain, where they had a good draft and lots of trees, which provided wood for the fire. After packing the furnace with chunks of limestone, the burnt, pulverized by-product helped restore the fertility of the soil by balancing the pH factor.

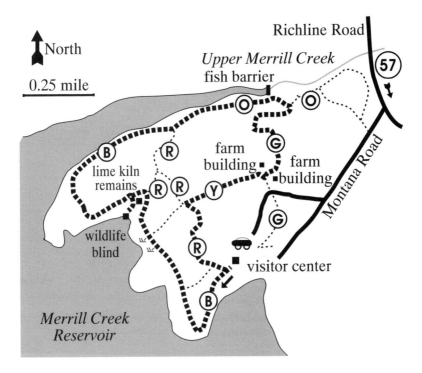

Woods surrounding Merrill Creek Reservoir

Turn left at the sign for a side trek to the wildlife observation blind at 0.9 mile. There is a good chance of spotting deer and birds in this area. Return to the main trail, turn left, and after another 0.3 mile, you'll be out in the open with a sweeping view of the reservoir ahead. The concrete building across the water is the 200-foot-high inlet-outlet tower used to control water flow. Asters and other wildflowers grow profusely in this area.

After climbing a short hill, you'll immediately descend into the woods again. At 1.4 miles, hundreds of dead trees stand submerged. After the reservoir basin was scoured out, it was stocked with fish and the trees were intentionally destroyed. It is hoped that better aquatic life will abound after the trees decay.

The trail is extremely rocky and difficult to negotiate for about 0.5 mile, but it's also quite interesting, with sweeping vistas of the reservoir and the sounds of birds as they fly close by.

After a few mini ups and downs, you'll reach a T. Turn left (at 1.9 miles) onto the orange-blazed Creek Trail. The route proceeds over low, wet areas through deep woods, following upper Merrill Creek and the northeast arm of the reservoir. In fall, the color of the leaves is dazzling!

At the map post at 2.3 miles, turn right onto the green-blazed Orchard Trail, continuing through some rocky areas under lush trees and shrubs. The trail leaves the forest and enters an abandoned orchard, part of the old Beers farm. Follow this trail as it changes to gravel past the Beers' old stone storage building, and through a large field. Turn right onto the level, yellow-blazed Historic Farmstead Trail at 2.7 miles. It soon changes into a dirt path. At the junction, turn left onto the red-blazed Timber Trail, which passes impressive pine plantations and hardwood forests in various stages. When you come into the open again, you'll spot a corner of the reservoir with the visitor center a short distance ahead.

36. Round Valley

Type:	Dayhike or overnight backpack
Difficulty:	Moderate for children
Distance:	6.5 miles, round trip
Elevation gain:	350 feet
Hikable:	Year-round
Hours:	8:00 A.M. to dark
Information:	Round Valley Recreation Area, Box 45-D, 1220 Lebanon–Stanton Rd., Lebanon 08833; (908) 236-6355
Admission:	Fee charged Memorial Day to Labor Day, except on Tuesdays; additional fee for overnight camping

Before 1958, Round Valley Reservoir didn't exist. There was, however, a natural horseshoe-shaped valley nestled in the rolling hills of Hunterdon County. Hardly anyone gave a thought to this hole in

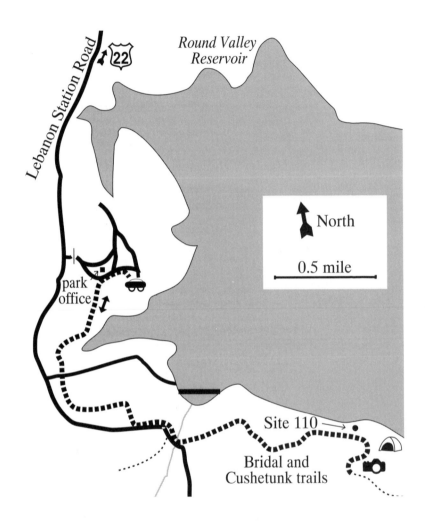

the ground—that is, until it was filled with 55 billion gallons of water. Today, the 70-foot-deep reservoir provides excellent recreational facilities, not to mention drinking water. Everyone enjoys the reservoir, from fishermen, who are hooked on the smallmouth bass, sunfish, and rainbow trout, to scuba divers, swimmers, picnickers, and boaters.

A year-round treasure, the reservoir also attracts those who love ice sports, cross-country skiing, and sledding. Best of all is the 9-mile-long hiking trail that leads to wilderness campsites accessible only by foot or boat. Make a reservation by mail or in person at the visitor center before starting the trip.

Ice sailing is one of the sports enjoyed during the winter at Round Valley.

From I-78 or NJ-22 southeast of Clinton, follow signs to the park office. Drive down a short distance to the diving area, the No. 1 parking lot.

The Bridal and Cushetunk trails begin at the bulletin board. Turn left and follow a green footprint blaze on a yellow background, walking away from the water. In a few yards, you'll reach the road; bear left, walking past pines and along a wide path with the water to your left. Just ahead, at 0.2 mile, you'll have the first of many fabulous views of the reservoir. The trail descends now, again leading to the water's edge; this is a popular fishing spot and a good place to observe the sailboats. Continuing, there are gradual ups and downs through pine woods. If you're here during spring, you'll see lots of evidence of the protective webs spun by tent caterpillars.

After crossing a road and walking through the fence opening at about 1 mile, a variety of birch, beech, and oak appear, with the water again visible to the left. Shortly, the trail becomes straight and level, with a wire fence a few yards ahead. As you descend, at 1.3 miles, there's an exceptional view of surrounding farmland and houses so far in the distance that they resemble toys. Turn left, cutting through the fence, and follow the trail sign that is about 0.1 mile farther on. To the left, at 1.6 miles, the grassy side of the dam appears. Cross the stream over a bridge made of concrete pipe, and climb steeply, still continuing along the fence. You'll have a chance to recover at 1.8 miles when the trail levels. Ahead, where the fence ends and the trail climbs again, is a stand of lovely cedars. The Bridal Trail sign comes in again, indicated by horseshoes on a yellow blaze. Occasionally you might have to move over to let a horse and rider through. Besides finding horseshoe prints, you may see various animal tracks belonging to deer, raccoons, opossums, red fox, and striped skunk. Even if you haven't seen any mammals, you'll definitely be able to hear and spot some of the birds that frequent the area. These include the beautiful rufous-sided towhee—an insect-eating bird with rust-colored sides, a white breast, and a long, rounded tail with large white spots, whose song is "drink-your-tea"—and the light-gray mockingbird, marked by spots of white on its tail and wings.

At 2.4 miles, turn left, climbing again. You can see the water in the distance as you head right. You'll see the water again over the treetops at 2.7 miles, with the best views during fall and summer. You'll reach the campsite toilets at about 3 miles; the wilderness campsite is a few feet farther. From this point, you can take a short walk down to the water or go on for another 0.25 mile to the scenic overlook, accessible from opposite the Wilderness Campground sign. This spot provides an overview of the reservoir. When you've drunk your fill of the panorama, continue to your campsite if you're spending the night; otherwise, follow the same trail back.

37. Black River Trail

Type:	Dayhike
Difficulty:	Easy for children
Distance:	3 miles, round trip
Elevation gain:	220 feet
Hikable:	Year-round
Hours:	Trails open 8:00 A.M.; call for closing hours
Information:	Hacklebarney State Park, 119 Hacklebarney Road, Long Valley 07853; (908) 638-6969
Admission:	Free; parking fee from Memorial Day to Labor Day

This is a kid's paradise! Our first trip here was in the dead of winter, when the tips of large boulders poked through a blanket of freshly fallen snow. Our boys couldn't resist scampering from one boulder to another and, to tell the truth, neither could we.

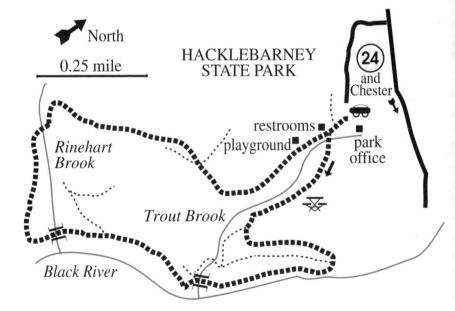

Situated along the Black River in a gorge of unusual beauty, Hacklebarney State Park lies primarily in a glacial valley. According to legend, it acquired its strange name from a local iron mine worker who persisted in heckling a foreman named Barney Tracey. Over a period of time, "heckle" Barney became "hacklebarney."

From Chester, drive west on NJ-24 3 miles, following signs to the park entrance.

Sturdy shoes are recommended. Take the trail from the parking area, turn left, and walk down the deep stone steps just beyond the restrooms to the first picnic area and Trout Brook. At first, it will probably be slow going because children always want to stop to toss rocks into the brook or spend time splashing near the waterfall. (Urge them to be careful; the rocks near the waterfall are quite slippery.) Once you're back on the trail, look for trees that have sprouted in cavities of other fallen trees. Now decayed, these "nurse logs" provide nutrients and a foundation for new growth.

Hemlocks are abundant in this 574-acre park because they're able

Picnic tables make a great rest stop for enjoying the sounds and sight of the fast-flowing Black River.

to survive in deep shade. During spring, Jack-in-the-pulpit thrives in the moist wooded areas near the river. American Indians used its pounded root to treat headaches. Jewelweed, whose flowers reflect light, resembling tiny jewels after a rainfall, also grows here. Some people claim it cures poison ivy if rubbed on the skin.

The trail meanders downhill to the Black River. Plan on lingering near the water, where the giant rocks lining the bank are a challenge to any child. In no time at all, the kids will be climbing on them, captivated by the fast-flowing river and fascinated by the many detours it takes around the rocks. (Again, use caution; these rocks are so high and uneven that a slip and fall could be quite serious.)

Follow the trail, keeping the river to your left. After crossing the second bridge, the trail ascends, curving away from the river and leading up a steep hill, past a playground, restrooms, and back to the parking area.

---

38. Jockey Hollow Ramble

Type:	Dayhike
Difficulty:	Moderate for children
Distance:	4.5 miles, round trip
Elevation gain:	250 feet
Hikable:	Year-round
Hours:	9:00 A.M. to sunset; closed holidays
Information:	Morristown National Historical Park, Washington Place, Morristown 07960; (973) 539-2085
Admission:	Fee; free with Golden Pass or National Parks Pass

George Washington's troops couldn't have appreciated this magnificent scenery. Drilling in freezing temperatures during the bitter winter of 1779–80 was enough to make any man miserable, and many of the 10,000 soldiers camped here perished for want of food, lack of clothing, and constant blizzards. Hiking on a sub-zero day may give you some idea of what they went through, but warm clothing, sturdy shoes, and trail mix to munch on make a big difference. So does having the time to enjoy the solitude, the flora and fauna, and the sights and sounds of a meandering stream. Plan on spending some time after the hike exploring Wick House, circa 1750; a ranger will describe how Henry Wick prospered by logging and farming his 800 acres of timberland and open fields and how the house was used by Major General Arthur St. Clair while he served as commander of the Pennsylvania Line.

 From NJ-202 north of Basking Ridge, take Tempe Wick Road west and follow signs to parking for the visitor center.

Exit from the rear of the visitor center, walk straight ahead on a wide, grassy path leading toward the Wick farm, and turn right at the split-rail fence. After crossing a blacktop road (watch for oncoming traffic), continue through the woods on a narrower, grassy trail. You'll pass a couple of signs explaining the historical events that occurred here; at the trail sign at about 0.25 mile, turn left onto Patriots' Path, designated by a blaze incorporating a winding river within a white circle. This area is a birdwatcher's paradise, largely due to the tall tulip trees that provide a generous seed supply. The trail becomes a series of ups and downs at about 0.5 mile, and when you're on the ridge and hear the sound of water, look down into the narrow gorge on the right. Eventually, you'll be walking next to that stream.

Look for the beeches that are mixed in with oaks, birches, and ashes. This handsome tree sports a light gray trunk, 3- to 6-inch-long sharp-toothed leaves, and thick toes at its base. Audubon thought so much of this tree that he used its bough as a background for his famous "Passenger Pigeon" painting. At the sign for the Primrose Trail

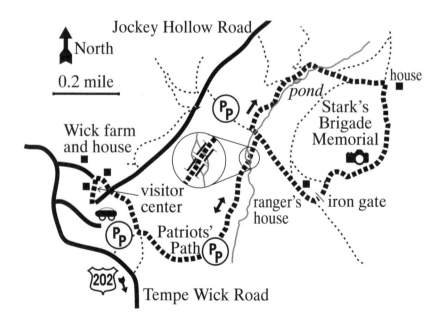

A split-rail fence leads to the Wick House and farm, a must-see after the hike.

and Grand Loop Trail, at about 1 mile, go straight on the Grand Loop Trail. Right after, cross over a wooden bridge. The next wooden bridge, a short distance ahead, is a great place to stop and admire the small stream as it meanders along.

Continue straight ahead, then turn left at the T at 1.3 miles, staying on Patriots' Path for a short while. After this, stay right at the next four trail intersections; trail maps, which will indicate your progress, are considerately placed at most of them. The first right turn comes up quickly and is marked by a double yellow blaze (at 1.4 miles). After climbing slightly, turn right again when the New York Brigade Trail signpost appears. In a couple of minutes, you'll be next to a small pond, which was a sheet of ice when we arrived. Turn right at the Mount Kemple Loop Trail post and again at the Y, following signs to Mount Kemple Loop Trail. When you reach the loop, turn left, following it in a clockwise direction.

After a gradual climb, you'll see the first sign of civilization, a house. Walk behind it, find the trail again, and right after the trail levels, you'll come to a memorial dedicated to Stark's Brigade. This slope afforded a perfect view of the valley and the Watchung Mountains (and still does). However, a mistake by the patrol could prove fatal, because it was difficult to distinguish between a patriot and a Tory. Patrolling these Watchung Mountains was referred to as duty "on the line."

After descending, turn left at the signpost for Camp Road Trail and turn right at the T, through an iron gate where thick vines have gotten a stranglehold on many of the trees. Go past the ranger's house, turn left at 3.3 miles before a wooden bridge, and head back on Patriots' Path the way you came. Turn right at a signpost for the Wick House and the visitor center.

39. Patriots' Path

Type:	Dayhike
Difficulty:	Moderate for children
Distance:	5 miles, round trip
Elevation gain:	300 feet
Hikable:	Year-round
Hours:	Trails, dawn to dusk; visitor center, daily May–Oct., 9:00 A.M.–5:00 P.M.; Nov.–Apr., call for times
Information:	Morristown National Historical Park, Washington Place, Morristown 07960; (973) 539-2085
Admission:	Free

In 1966, Helen C. Fenske proposed the creation of a corridor to link parklands and historic sites from Mendham Township through Morristown. A name was needed, and historian/writer John T. Cunningham came up with Patriots' Path. The name is fitting because you'll be following in the footsteps of General George Washington and his Continental Army as you go through Jockey Hollow Park. If you'd like to be all alone, try coming during the week. The trail leads past where the troops camped, and one of their stone hearths still remains. Afterward, stop in at Wick House to learn how Henry Wick worked his 800 acres of timberland and open field, until the army felled the trees to build huts and fuel fires to keep the men warm during the coldest winter recorded in the eighteenth century.

From NJ-202 north of Basking Ridge, take Tempe Wick Road west and follow signs to visitor center parking.

Exit from the rear of the visitor center, walk straight ahead on a wide, grassy path leading toward the Wick farm, and turn right at the split-rail fence. After crossing a blacktop road (watch for oncoming traffic), continue through the woods on a narrower, grassy trail. You'll pass a couple of signs at about 0.25 mile explaining the historical events that occurred here during the bitter winter of 1779–80. At the trail junction sign at about 0.25 mile, turn right onto Patriots' Path, which is designated by a blaze incorporating a winding river within a white circle, and head downhill on the rocky path.

Skunk cabbage, known for its strong, unpleasant odor at close range, pops its green spathe through the snow as early as February. It grows profusely in the marshy areas next to the melodious stream at about 0.4 mile. Listed in the *United States Pharmacopeia* in the 1800s, skunk cabbage was used to treat a host of illnesses, including epilepsy and asthma. It might also have been one of the first contraceptives, because those indulging in a daily dose believed it caused sterility.

In a couple of minutes you'll cross Tempe Wick Road; watch for passing cars. Shortly, you'll cross a wooden bridge over a stream flanked with boulders, ferns, and more skunk cabbage. A downed tree here can serve as a bench if you'd like to enjoy the peaceful surroundings before the long uphill climb ahead. At 0.9 mile, you'll descend gradu-

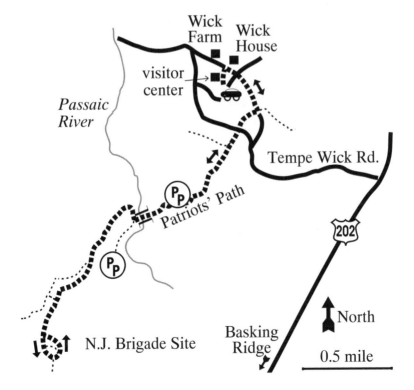

The dense woods and cool streams make for a delightful hike year-round.

ally, passing a field of low green weeds. As the trail narrows and meanders through hundreds of trees, you'll hear songbirds chattering, and if you're lucky, you will spot one of the resident owls.

Pause on the bridge across the Passaic River to watch the waters flowing past boulders and downed trees. Then cross the river, turn right, and continue uphill; at the top of the hill, at just under 2 miles, turn left, and continue following the sign for the N.J. Brigade site. The path remains level for a few yards before gradually ascending again. Stay left at the trail junction sign at 2.1 miles, proceeding gradually downhill in a few yards. At the next trail junction signs, at 2.6 miles, turn left, going slightly uphill to the Brigade site, where the troops endured bitter weather and a lack of food and clothing. From here, continue uphill a short distance to see the remains of a hearth left over from one of the soldier's huts. Those huts stood 14 by 16 feet square and 6½ feet high. The stone fireplaces were for cooking and heating. In 1780, 1,200 huts standing 2 feet apart had been built in Jockey Hollow. By the time the troops moved on, 900 acres of trees had been destroyed in the surrounding area.

Continue climbing steeply from here, and at the T junction with Patriots' Path (3.2 miles), turn right and return to the start.

40. Dogwood Trail (Scherman-Hoffman Sanctuaries)

Type: Dayhike
Difficulty: Easy for children
Distance: 2.1 miles, round trip
Elevation gain: 260 feet
Hikable: Year-round
Hours: Trails, daily to 5:00 P.M.
Information: P.O. Box 693, 11 Hardscrabble Road, Bernardsville 07924; (908) 766-5787
Admission: Free

The ridges and valleys in this area, formed approximately 600 million years ago, were just what General George Washington was looking for. Because the ridges didn't have any natural passes, the enemy could be spotted far in advance, which allowed the troops to rest. Today, this hike leads through lush woods and an old farm field loaded with butterflies, wildflowers, and woodchucks and along the banks of the Passaic River. Deer, especially active an hour before sunset, are abundant.

Take NJ-287 to Exit 26, Basking Ridge. Use the westbound exit, continuing through the traffic light at NJ-202. The road name becomes Childs Road. Bear right at the fork on Hardscrabble Road for about 1 mile and turn right at the sign to the Hoffman parking lot.

Begin on the Field Loop Trail, next to the Hoffman House. This hike takes a couple of hours to complete, depending on how many times the kids are tempted to peek beneath fallen logs or climb boulders.

The trail descends slightly for 0.2 mile until it reaches a trail junction; turn left onto the red-blazed Dogwood Trail, which gradually climbs uphill passing through thick stands of beech, birch, oak, tulip, and maple trees. At approximately 0.75 mile, turn left at the top of the ridge and continue following the red blazes where the trail descends past rock formations. Caution: When you reach the enormous sinkhole, walk single file; the leaves can be slippery and it's a long way down. A quarter mile farther look for the "elephant rock," which is actually a twisted tree that has merged with the rock over time. When the tree was young, it was forced to grow around the rock, forming a shape like an elephant's trunk.

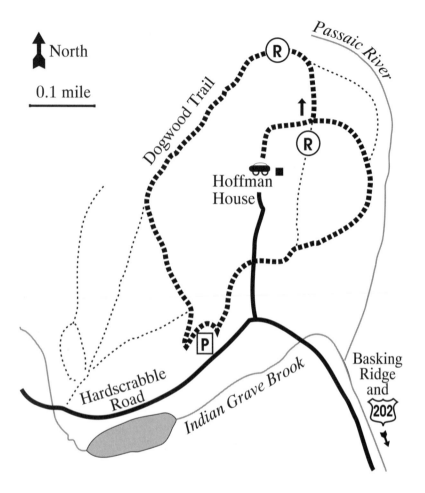

You'll come to another parking lot in 0.25 mile, but continue climbing again until you cross a road. Go straight ahead (on the Field Loop Trail). Old farm equipment lies rusting on the right; to the left, a tree identification chart lists varieties found in this area, including dogwood, shagbark hickory, sugar maple, and tulip. Woodchucks and butterflies favor this section, and can often be spotted munching on blackeyed susan and goldenrod. You'll hear and see lots of birds, and will pass cutouts leading to the Passaic River—a great place for the kids to watch for birds and deer.

Proceed uphill to return to the parking lot, but before leaving, stop in at the Hoffman House to examine the many interesting exhibits and a gift shop filled with bird feeders, books, and items pertaining to the outdoors.

Fascinating tree formations—such as this one, which has sprouted from atop a split rock—await along the Dogwood Trail.

41. Loantaka Reservation

Type:	Dayhike
Difficulty:	Easy for children
Distance:	3.5 miles, round trip
Elevation gain:	Negligible
Hikable:	Year-round
Hours:	Dawn to dusk
Information:	Morris County Park Commission, P.O. Box 1295, Morristown 07962; (973) 326-7600
Admission:	Free

One of the highlights of this pleasant hike is crossing a shallow stream. While it's a snap to maintain your balance stepping across carefully laid stones, many children love to "accidentally" fall in. Don't worry if they do; only their shoes and socks will get wet.

Used by hikers and bikers, the well-maintained paved trail me-

A low spot on the trail creates a pleasant obstacle.

North

0.25 mile

Loantaka Way

Loantaka Brook

Gibbons horse barn

Stepping-Stone Bridge

Spring Valley Road

Kitchell Pond

Kitchell Road

(24) and Morristown

anders through a narrow strip of woodland that's particularly pleasing during autumn, when fallen leaves create a golden carpet. Hungry ducks and Canada geese wait for a handout at Kitchell Pond.

From I-287 exit at NJ-24 in Morristown, head east on South Street, and then turn left on Spring Valley Road and left again on Loantaka Way, to a parking area on the left.

Take the paved trail at the left of the map in the parking area. Continue straight ahead at the crossing. At 0.5 mile, you'll cross a small bridge over the first of several streams. Skunk cabbage, named for its offensive odor, is abundant in the wet areas. Because this plant produces heat as it grows, it's one of the first wildflowers to poke its coiled bright green spathe through the ground, and can even pop up through snow.

The trail continues through woods, with no significant elevation change. Take the "stepping-stone" bridge over Loantaka Brook at 1.25 miles, and at about 1.5 miles, use caution in crossing Kitchell Road to reach Kitchell Pond.

Allow time for exploration of the pond and small footbridge before returning the way you came. Turn right at the trail junction (2.7 miles). In a few yards, to the right you'll see a huge downed tree resting over the stream. A bit farther are outstanding examples of the tree responsible for the spokes used in yesteryear's wagon wheels and today's ax handles—the shagbark hickory. As the name implies, this tree has loose bark standing out from the trunk. Deer are a common sight in this area, especially late in the day.

After crossing through a safety gate, turn left and continue along the road for about 0.25 mile to the parking lot. Caution: Keep to the extreme left side of the road to avoid oncoming traffic. To the right is the Gibbons horse barn, circa 1834, built by William Gibbons to house his thoroughbred racehorses, including Fashion, once known as the "Queen of the American Turf."

42. Lord Stirling Park

Type:	Dayhike
Difficulty:	Easy for children
Distance:	3.9 miles, round trip
Elevation gain:	Negligible
Hikable:	Year-round, buggy in summer
Hours:	Center, daily 9:00 A.M.–5:00 P.M.; trails for permit holders, dawn to dusk; otherwise 9:00 A.M.–5:00 P.M.
Information:	190 Lord Stirling Road, Basking Ridge 07920; (908) 766-2489
Admission:	Free; hikers without an annual permit (fee) must register at the center

Children are often reluctant to walk one step farther when they get to the start of the trail—they'd much rather admire the antics of the Canada geese in manmade Branta Pond. Who can blame them?

The beauty and constant "honk-honk" chatter of these creatures is exhilarating. However, there are many more treasures to be found on these easy, level trails within the 400 acres of Lord Stirling Park. Deer, meadow voles, and rabbits are frequent visitors on the 1,200-foot-long circular path that skirts the pond. This trail is a pleasant warm-up for the more interesting things to come. A magnifying glass is helpful for examining insect-eating plants in the boggy area, one of five major plant communities in the park.

If you love birds, bring binoculars; you'll probably also spot deer, pheasants, raccoons, skunks, opossum, and sometimes fox. Nearly 8,000 feet of boardwalk extend over the high-water areas. One section leads to a tall tower in a remote, marshy bend of the Passaic River. Plan on having lunch here; you'll never forget the experience of looking

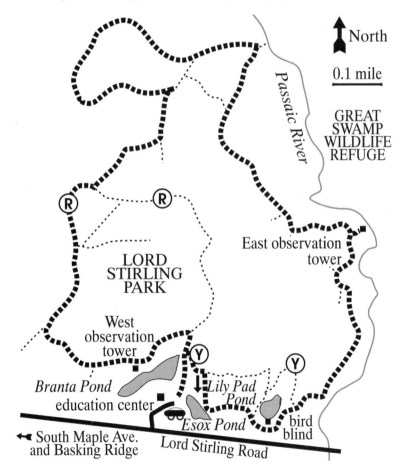

Wonderful trails await hikers at Lord Stirling Park.

out to the east at the quiet, mysterious depths of the Great Swamp National Wildlife Refuge. During spring, chain pickerel flip out of the water, briefly suspended in midair, as they journey upstream into the swamps and marshes where they spawn. There are also spring beauties such as trillium and lady's slipper, nine species of nonpoisonous snakes, and turtles (don't handle any; they may bite). When you arrive back at the Environmental Education Center, spend some time examining the seasonal displays in this 18,000-square-foot solar-heated and -cooled building, the first of its kind in the nation. It's also a good idea to pick up a trail map here.

The land you'll be hiking on was originally owned by William Alexander or, as he insisted on being addressed, "Lord Stirling." To claim his title, Alexander had to visit England, but the British House of Lords nevertheless refused to acknowledge him. Despite this one vanity, Alexander was a man of great accomplishment; he not only served as surveyor general and one of Columbia University's founders, but also gave his last dollar to outfit the New Jersey militia.

A variety of owners occupied this land after Lord Stirling's death in 1783. Then, in the 1970s, with the possibility of a jet port being built on these grounds, the Somerset County Park Commission purchased the property and built the Environmental Education Center "to educate the people about open space values and public land use management."

From Basking Ridge, go south on South Maple Avenue, turn left on Lord Stirling Road, and proceed to the park entrance.

The entrance is to the right of the Environmental Education Center, via a straight gravel path dividing Branta Pond from Esox Pond. A short distance away is an information gazebo describing how the surrounding land, the Great Swamp, was formed. During fall, the field ahead is aglow with an enormous variety of wildflowers, including daisies, chicory, and Queen Anne's lace. Children are usually amazed to learn how important these wildflowers are to field dwellers. Moths, butterflies, and bees prize the nectar, while birds dine on the seeds and strip the leaves to line their nests. Just before the woods, look on the right side of the trail (around 0.2 mile) for a post with yellow reflectors, which indicates a right turn onto the yellow trail. (There will be a series of trail junctions; bear right at each one until you hit the red trail.) Don't be surprised if a huge bird, the great blue heron, flies overhead as you approach. Most likely, it was looking for a tasty morsel in Esox Pond, just ahead.

From this area, there's an excellent view of the education center. A bird blind is located at about 0.4 mile; if the food boxes are filled, you'll spot some beauties. From here, the wide, grassy trail leads to the edge of Lily Pad Pond, another good viewing area. The next right turn takes you off the yellow trail and into deep woods at 0.5 mile.

Beautiful wildflowers, such as this red trillium, carpet the forest floor during spring.

The topography changes from woods to open field and back again. After another right turn at about 0.9 mile, grasses appear; these can be hypnotizing when they sway in the slightest breeze. In the spring, have children study a blade of grass under a magnifying glass. They'll see that grasses actually bloom!

After a long walk on the boardwalk, you'll reach the east observation tower at 1 mile. The climb up the staircase is steep, but the view is magnificent.

Walk back to the trail and turn right. At about 1.2 miles, the woods become so dense that it almost feels like evening. The trail enters a wetter region, and then a boardwalk appears at 1.5 miles that meanders through wooded areas and open fields. Turn right when the boardwalk divides and go past a field of cattails. Kids usually like to hear about how their parents smoked these "punks" when they were children, and about how the Indians prepared cereal by chopping the pretty stalk. At 1.7 miles, take a right for another close-up view of the Passaic River. When finished examining the mushrooms and lichens that thrive in this peaceful area, turn around and continue, still keeping to the right when the trail forks. The trail goes through woods and over more wet sections. At about 2 miles, a boardwalk goes over a stagnant body of water with a crust of thick algae, bright yellow waterlilies, and hundreds of cattails. This is one section of boardwalk that truly delights children; they love hopping over the sections that are partially submerged, and even like getting their feet wet!

In another 0.25 mile, you'll arrive at a junction with three boardwalks. Turn right as usual and continue for an additional 0.25 mile to a junction with the red trail. From this point, follow the red markings back to the Environmental Education Center. The swampy section encountered at 3 miles is eerie; hundreds of cattails appear, along with dead wood sticking up all around. The trail passes the west observation blind before skirting open field. At the T, turn right, cross over the bridge, and head toward the center.

43. Great Swamp

Type:	Dayhike
Difficulty:	Easy for children
Distance:	2.5 miles, round trip
Elevation gain:	Negligible
Hikable:	Fall and winter are best, when ground is drier
Hours:	Dawn to dusk
Information:	Refuge Manager, Great Swamp National Wildlife Refuge, 152 Pleasant Plains Road, Basking Ridge 07920; (973) 425-1222
Admission:	Free

When English investors purchased 30,000 acres of land from the Delaware Indians in 1708 for a barrel of rum, four pistols, fifteen kettles, thirty pounds sterling, and other miscellaneous items, they

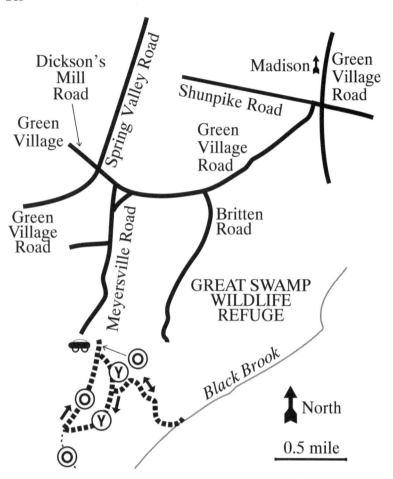

probably went away laughing. But the Indians felt pretty good too, knowing that a good portion of the land sold was under water!

Settlements sprang up quickly, and during the Revolutionary War, wood was collected from the upland areas for making wagon wheels. After draining the marshlands in 1844, foul meadow hay became the major cash crop. When farming was no longer profitable, the land was abandoned, and it slowly reverted to woods and swampland.

All was quiet until 1959, when the threat of building a jet port in the area known as the Great Swamp aroused concern. Raising over a million dollars, groups of local citizens purchased 3,000 acres and donated it to the U.S. Department of the Interior. This formed the nucleus of the Great Swamp National Wildlife Refuge, and in 1968, Congress designated the area as part of the National Wilderness Preservation System. Through the years, additional acres have been added.

More than 200 species of birds have been spotted in the refuge, as well as a variety of mammals including the white-tailed deer, woodchuck, beaver, raccoon, and muskrat. While traversing though woodland and cattail marsh, imagine how this area was created about 25,000 years ago when the Wisconsin Glacier stopped abruptly on its way south. As it melted, long ridges of sand and gravel were left behind, blocking the outlet of an ancient river basin. Eventually, a huge lake formed, although it was drained when the retreating glacier created a second outlet. What remained were marshes and swamp.

From Madison, take Green Village Road southwest toward Green Village. Turn left on Meyersville Road to the end and park.

Waterproof shoes or boots are advisable, except when the ground is frozen or when it's been unusually dry. Walk through the fence opening in front of the parking area to a trail marked by orange blazes. When you come to a short boardwalk in a few yards you may hear the throaty song of red-winged blackbirds or the tapping of downy woodpeckers. At about 0.2 mile, turn left onto a trail with yellow markings. Almost immediately, you'll see a carpet of club moss, a green flowerless plant that thrives in this damp environment. Look at its finely toothed leaves and spores with a magnifying glass.

At about 0.5 mile, a double blaze indicates that the trail divides; bear left and walk southeast. If you pause a couple of minutes at one of the rotting logs, you'll find lots of wildlife and plants. Salamanders

A boardwalk keeps this hiker high and dry through swamp and outstanding cattails.

The Great Swamp during winter, an ideal time to visit because it's free of insects—but wear boots or waterproof shoes.

like the moist area underneath a log, while deer mice and squirrels prefer the cozier interior of the log for raising their families. When the winter wind blows through the large beeches at 0.75 mile, the last of the leaves stubbornly clinging to the branches emit a shivering sound as they dance in the breeze.

Black Brook, to the right of the trail at 0.9 mile, is a fine place to find ducks and Canada geese. At the trail's end a short distance later, double back the way you came, and after reaching the double yellow blaze at 1.4 miles, turn left and walk southwest. Cattails surround the boardwalk at 1.8 miles. Indians had many uses for that freshwater plant: They ate the young shoots, wove its leaves into mats, dipped the seed heads in fat to make torches, and used the fluffy seeds for quilt stuffing and insulation.

Turn right at the T a short distance ahead and walk northeast on the orange-blazed trail. (For a longer walk, turn left instead and then return.) Tall spruces appear just ahead; leave the trail for a few minutes to wander among them. When ready, return to the trail and continue back to the parking area.

44. Mills Reservation

Type: Dayhike
Difficulty: Easy for children
Distance: 2 miles, round trip
Elevation gain: 100 feet
Hikable: Year-round; best birding in spring and fall
Hours: Dawn to dusk
Information: Essex County Department of Parks, 115 Clifton Avenue, Newark 07104; (973) 268-3500
Admission: Free

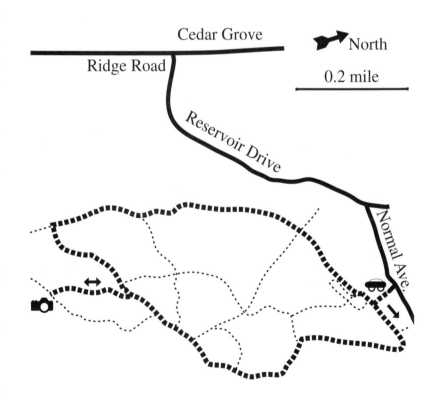

Mythology tells of giants, demons, and dragons lurking deep in the heart of the woods. However, as far back as anyone can remember, people have found safety, food, and shelter in the forest. The same holds true today, and thanks to a donation of 157 acres of woodland by the Davela Mills Foundation in 1954, hikers can also enjoy peace and quiet on these trails despite the fact that the reservation is located between the crowded surburbs of Cedar Grove and Upper Montclair.

You'll reach an overlook affording an excellent view of Manhattan, Staten Island, and Newark, and if you arrive during migration in spring and fall, chances are you'll spot one of fourteen species of birds.

In Cedar Grove take Ridge Road and turn east onto Reservoir Drive and then right onto Normal Avenue for 0.25 mile to the parking lot on the right.

Leaving the parking lot, walk uphill on the gravel trail and turn left at the fork. The trail heads slightly downhill at 0.4 mile for about 0.25 mile. Turn left at the fork and leave the loop trail at 0.7 mile, going slightly uphill. Oak and hickory are dominant, with a good showing of birch, tulip, and beech throughout this area.

You'll reach the observation point and the remains of an old stone foundation at 0.9 mile. If you've brought binoculars, they'll come in handy for peering at hawks, the tiny American kestrel, or even a bald eagle.

Sassafras reflects a recent rain.

When ready, turn back the way you came, but use caution; there are some steep drops along these cliffs. At the fork, turn left heading downhill. The red oaks growing here were highly valued for the tannic acid in their bark by the leather industry that sprang up in the area. Turn right at the T. Continue straight on the gravel trail that leads uphill at 1.7 miles, but soon levels out. Hair cap moss, found throughout this area, may be curled up if the weather's been dry, but sprinkle a little water on it and watch it unfold. At the T where you first came onto the loop trail (1.9 miles), turn left and continue back to the parking lot.

45. Turtle Back

Type: Dayhike
Difficulty: Easy for children
Distance: 2.25 miles, round trip
Elevation gain: 200 feet
Hikable: Year-round
Hours: Dawn to dusk
Information: Essex County Department of Parks, 115 Clifton Avenue, Newark 07104; (973) 268-3500
Admission: Free

It wasn't possible to hike through the South Mountain Reservation 200 million years ago because of the erupting volcanoes. After the boiling lava spewed out and cooled down, the land tilted upward, leaving hard and soft layers of basalt and sandstone exposed. As the sandstone eroded, the basalt layers formed three ridges. Much, much later, they came to be known by the Lenape Indians as the "Wach Unks," meaning "high hills."

Two of these ridges that we know today as the Watchung Mountains lie within the reservation's 2,048 acres, a unique stretch of public land offering 19 miles of hiking trails. While hiking through the southeastern corner, you'll see small waterfalls and the Orange Reservoir. Thanks to the efforts of the Essex County Park Commission, you'll also be hiking through dense woods, planted in 1895 to restore the natural woodland that had been stripped by logging mills in the

North

0.25 mile

Northfield Avenue

Prospect Ave.
West Orange

Walker Avenue

Cherry Lane

carriage road

Orange
Reservoir

Longwood Road

SOUTH MOUNTAIN
RESERVATION

South
Orange
Avenue

1750s, and later by the paper industry, which chopped down second-growth forest. Hemlock and white pine were replanted, along with an understory of mountain laurel and wild azalea. Over 3,000 rhododendron were planted in 1910 for the grand sum of forty-three cents each!

 From I-280 in West Orange take Prospect Avenue south, turn right on Northfield Avenue, and left on Walker Road. Make the first right turn into the South Mountain Reservation and park.

The parking area is located atop Turtle Back Rock, a name that aptly describes the shape of this huge rock plateau. Walk southwest to the end of the parking lot through the picnic area, and head west. Tall oaks and beeches are abundant, but if children are along, ask them to walk very quietly for a while. They'll probably spot a toad or turtle in the hollow of a tree or beneath a pile of brush. As you go deeper into the woods, look for mosses, the flowerless green plants that hug the forest floor and old stumps, as well as the mushrooms (fungi) and lichens (combinations of an alga and a fungus) that thrive

Always be on the lookout for poison ivy and remember: "Leaves of three, let it be."

in damp places. When you reach the orange blazes identifying the Turtle Back Trail, turn left bearing south. The trail soon narrows and crosses over a tiny stream. Climb slightly, heading left at 0.8 mile, and continue along the side of a beautiful ravine, using caution; the often slippery trail slants toward a dropoff. Boulders of every size and shape lie scattered below. The trail levels out at about 0.9 mile and then there are a couple of ups and downs. Bear right at the fork at 1 mile, heading steeply downhill. Blazes do not appear too frequently in this area, so be careful not to lose the trail.

From this ridge, Orange Reservoir appears to the right. At a triple blaze, bear right on the orange trail, proceeding downhill a few feet after crossing the stream. At the T at about 1.3 miles, turn right onto the wide carriage trail. The 20 miles of carriage roads traversing the reservation are heavily used not only for hiking, but also for jogging, horseback riding, and cross-country skiing. Orange Reservoir is now on the left.

In a few feet, you'll come to a tiny, but pretty waterfall that sounds especially melodious after a rainshower. The trail ascends at 1.4 miles. After a couple of dips and rises, there's a long uphill section; continue following the orange blazes. When you reach the double orange blazes at 2 miles, turn right, heading uphill and then left, back to Turtle Back Rock and the parking area.

46. Hemlock Falls

Type:	Dayhike
Difficulty:	Moderate for children
Distance:	5.25 miles, round trip
Elevation gain:	440 feet
Hikable:	Year-round
Hours:	Dawn to dusk
Information:	Essex County Department of Parks, 115 Clifton Avenue, Newark 07104; (973) 268-3500
Admission:	Free

Thanks to the Sierra Club, the yellow-blazed Lenape Trail will eventually cover 36 miles and link dozens of county, municipal, and historical areas. This hike begins on the first completed segment at the western corner of the South Mountain Reservation, and rambles over the same land George Washington surveyed during the Revolution. He realized the mountain range we know today as the Watchungs would offer his troops perfect cover from the British.

You'll be crossing many scenic streams, where you'll see water tumbling over boulders. Hemlock Falls creates an impressive cascade, especially after heavy rain or snowmelt. There are also scenic overlooks and dense woods chock-full of plants and wildlife.

 The hike begins at a parking area off the intersection of Glen Street and Lackawanna Place in Millburn, about a block northeast from the railroad station.

Near the start, several trails merge. Take the second from the left, an old carriage road. As you gradually ascend this rocky trail that follows the ridge, you'll see an old quarry below. At about 0.3 mile, turn right at the T, then left, following the yellow-blazed Lenape Trail. A deep, lush ravine appears in another 0.3 mile, where you'll hear the melodious sound of Maple Falls long before you see it. Cross a small stream and head uphill along the narrow, rocky trail. Stands of green-leafed mountain laurel stand out on even the bleakest winter's day.

After crossing Pingry Road (closed to traffic), and before climbing again, you'll pass more inviting streams. Where the trail descends and widens, there is new growth, and after the trees have shed their leaves, the view of the surrounding country is outstanding. The sound of gently flowing water is heard once more at 1.6 miles, especially after a heavy

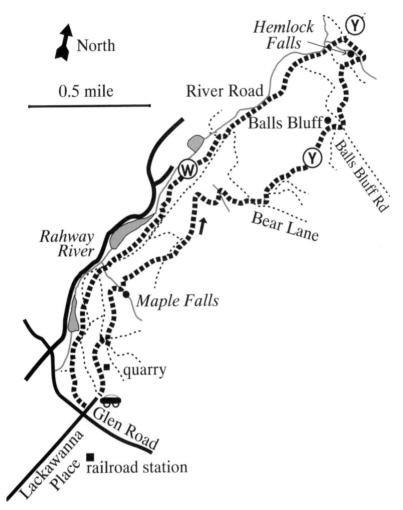

rain or when the snow is melting. The small waterfall (Maples Falls) just ahead makes a peaceful spot to rest or listen to the birds. It's also a good place to turn around if you don't feel like going on to Hemlock Falls.

To continue, proceed uphill and cross a dirt road (Bear Lane) at 1.9 miles. Pause for a few minutes when you reach Ball's Bluff and the remains of a shelter erected by the Civilian Conservation Corps (CCC) in 1934. The stone support columns are all that have survived. The trail descends steeply from this point, crosses Balls Bluff Road (a carriage road), and leads to an area with downed trees, mountain laurel, and a stream. Keeping your balance on the natural rock bridge across the stream at 2.9 miles is lots of fun; this leads to a short uphill section, which then bears left on a narrow trail leading to a beautiful stand of rhododendron. Cross another old road and then a bridge near Hemlock Falls. The trail turns left and follows a carriage road for a short distance. Leave the trail when it turns right, and stay on the road. After crossing a bridge, continue straight ahead along the wide path (River Road). Several feet ahead is a magnificent spot to admire the Rahway River.

The trail is now level and wide, with dense woods providing a lovely backdrop for the stream. The sound of the flowing water can be heard even when the river temporarily disappears from view. Beautiful hemlocks tower overhead. Turn right on the wide path, an old carriage road, at about 3.8 miles, and then make a quick left onto the white-blazed Rahway Trail. The path goes by small ponds, good places for youngsters to try their skill at skipping rocks. Lush rhododendron surround the trail in about another 0.2 mile. Delightful woods and water continue to work their magic; but gradually, you hear hints of civilization's return as you follow the path back to the starting point.

Getting ready for the trail ahead

47. Watchung Reservation

Type: Dayhike
Difficulty: Moderate for children
Distance: 2.4 miles, round trip
Elevation gain: 150 feet
Hikable: Year-round
Hours: Dawn to dusk
Information: Trailside Nature and Science
Center, Coles Avenue and
New Providence Road,
Mountainside 07092;
(908) 789-3670
Admission: Free

Sunglasses hadn't been invented when the Lenape Indians roamed these woods. Fortunately, they didn't need them. Neither will you, thanks to the natural shade provided by tall trees in the Watchung Reservation. The Lenapes referred to the area that lies between two ridges as the "Wach Unks," meaning "high hills." We know them today as the Watchung Mountains.

On the trails, you'll be able to spot deer, birds, and wildflowers while walking beside a beautiful babbling brook. An added bonus is passing through the remains of Feltville, a village ruled by David Felt.

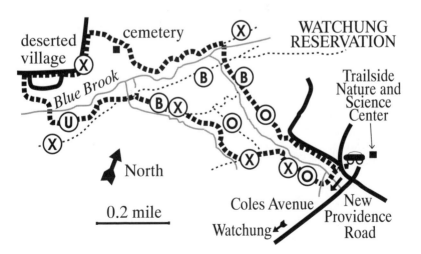

Nicknamed the "king" by his employees in this paper manufacturing village, Felt ruled with an iron hand, demanding that everyone live on his property, shop in his general store, and attend the church he built for them. Felt even sounded a bell when it was time for them to retire for the evening!

After the hike, plan on exploring the Trailside Nature and Science Center, adjacent to the parking area, where you can take in a nature film, lecture, or planetarium show.

 From Watchung, take Valley Road north and continue straight ahead on Sky Top Drive and then Coles Avenue. Turn left into the parking lot for the Trailside Nature and Science Center.

Walk away from the center on the blacktop road leading downhill, to the trail signs on the left side of the road. Follow the Sierra Trail, indicated by an "X" blaze, and go slightly uphill for a few yards. The narrow trail, also marked with green triangles, levels in a couple of yards, and Blue Brook can be heard at approximately 0.1 mile. Oaks and tulip trees tower overhead, and the area is always alive with birds. An orange-blazed trail joins in, just after a left turn. Examine the growth on the forest floor for evidence that life does, indeed, go on after death: Mushrooms grow profusely on fallen trees.

The trail turns to the right at 0.3 mile, but this is easy to miss because it isn't well-marked. After walking slightly downhill, there's a muddy section that soon levels out; a gully will be on the left. The blue trail joins in at 0.6 mile. Exercise caution and hold on to little ones at this point; there's a steep dropoff into the gully on the left. Still following the Sierra Trail, cross over the stream at 0.7 mile; at the other side, leave the marked trail and take the right fork onto an unmarked path. To the right is a fantastic view of Blue Brook. The next few downhill yards are slippery. The trail soon follows the brook, a perfect place to stop to play, wade, or look for wildlife. As the trail climbs up the hillside, it becomes slippery again; use caution. At the top of the hill (0.9 mile), bear right. You'll be following along the brook again, where, during late winter, skunk cabbage pokes up from the ground. This remote area is very peaceful, but one where you can easily get lost. You may have to bushwhack, bearing in mind that the stream should be kept on the right. Cross the bridge over the brook at 1 mile. As soon as you reach the other side, look for a trail going up the ridge to see the remains of Feltville, now referred to as the Deserted Village.

Turn right onto the paved road at 1.1 mile, where the Sierra Trail joins in again, and follow it to Felt's combination residence, church, and post office—all that remains of his reign, which at one point included thirteen double houses, two dormitories for single men and women, a manor house, a school, a barn, and a blacksmith shop. The paper manufacturing venture thrived until 1860, when he tired of running the operation and people started moving away.

Proceed uphill through the village. A few yards after the last house, follow the Sierra Trail, which goes right where the road continues straight at 1.4 miles, into the woods. Turn right in a few feet and follow the double blaze to a cemetery where members of the Wilcox family are buried. Peter Wilcox, a Dutch settler, erected a gristmill and lumber mill here in the 1700s; during the American Revolution and the War of 1812, the mill was converted into a gunpowder plant.

Walk downhill, away from the cemetery, and take the right fork onto an old road at 1.9 miles, leaving the Sierra Trail. Cross the brook, and at another junction take the middle path leading to the blue-blazed trail. The orange-blazed trail joins in at 2.1 miles, climbing gradually to reach the paved road. Turn right to return to the parking area.

Climbing over rocks is always a challenge.

48. Cheesequake Cedar Swamp Trail

Type:	Dayhike
Difficulty:	Easy for children
Distance:	2.7 miles, round trip
Elevation gain:	200 feet
Hikable:	Year-round
Hours:	Dawn to dusk
Information:	Cheesequake State Park, Matawan 07747; (732) 566-2161
Admission:	Free; fee for parking Memorial Day through Labor Day and for camping

Opened in 1940, Cheesequake State Park is Middlesex County's only state park. It lies between New Jersey's northern and southern vegetation zones, making it a transitional area with unique plant and animal life over a diversity of terrain.

While hiking the green-blazed Cedar Swamp Trail, the longest in the park, you'll have close-up views of pine barrens similar to those in the southern part of the state; a freshwater swamp with outstanding specimens of Atlantic white cedar, sweetbay magnolia, and red maple; and a mature hardwood forest where American beech, black birch, and white and red oak predominate. Over 186 species of birds have been sighted in these woods, as well as many mammals, including red foxes, white-tailed deer, and chipmunks.

There's still lots of speculation about how the park was named. Some believe its origin is from the Indian word "chichequaas," meaning "upland village." But, because Cheesequake lies on a fault where tectonic movement has been recorded as recently as 1979, others think it was named because the earth trembles like cheese! When you explore the quaking bogs in the marshes, you may agree with this version.

 From Matawan, take NJ-34 north, turn right on Disbrow Road, and right again at the T on Morristown Road to the park entrance. Alternatively, take the Garden State Parkway to Exit 120 and follow signs leading into the park. Continue straight, past the entrance booth less than 0.1 mile ahead, to the trail parking area on the left.

Start from the trail map in the parking area, head gradually downhill, and turn left at 0.1 mile, following red and green blazes. After crossing a brook and a slight rise, you'll reach the interpretive center; this is an excellent place to learn about the flora and fauna of the area before continuing on the sandy, level trail. Mountain laurel, abundant in this area, provides a lush green backdrop against the fallen snow in winter, while its pink blooms burst with a dazzling display each spring.

After descending for a few more yards, a boardwalk will take you over a wet area where skunk cabbage abounds. Although it has a rank odor, its spathe (large, enveloping, green, stalklike leaf) is quite attractive. Sphagnum moss, resembling a rich, bright green carpet, also thrives in this swampy section.

Fern and mitten-shaped sassafras appear a short distance ahead. After a series of easy ups and downs, bear right where the trail divides, following the green blazes. Take the steep stairs at 0.8 mile, but hold

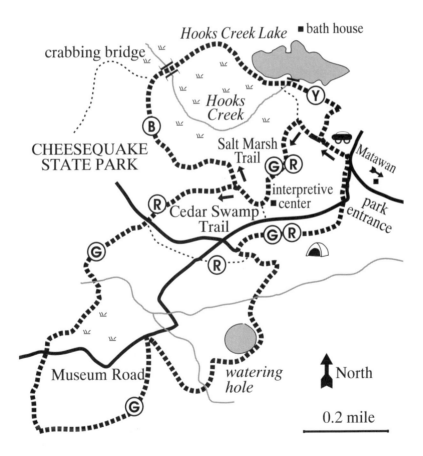

Boardwalks lead hikers over the wet areas in the swampy section of the trail.

 on to little ones; sand between the steps makes them slippery. You'll immediately be on a level boardwalk, which will keep your feet dry in this wet area. You're now entering the dark, mysterious Atlantic cedar swamp, where sweetbay magnolia, swamp azalea, and highland blueberry thrive. The fallen cedar logs are still intact after many years, due to the acidic soil that slows down decay. Woodpeckers hunting for insects within the dead trees are frequent visitors, and if you come late in the day, you may be lucky enough to spot a great horned owl.

The tall, century-old white pines nearby are a treat for the eyes and the nose. During the 1600s, the British Crown took the straightest, tallest trees and used them as masts for the Royal Navy's ships, but when the American Revolution began, their supply was cut off. White pine is still used for building and furniture.

Take a deep breath for the steepest climb of this hike at 1.3 miles. Fortunately, it's short, leveling after a few yards. Deer sometimes hang out at the watering hole on the left at 2 miles; early in the morning or evening are good times to be here. A bit past this spot, try your balancing act while walking over the fallen logs.

You'll be out in the open at 2.4 miles, at the group campsite. The trail, indicated by red and green blazes, leads back into the woods in a few more yards. If you didn't stop at the interpretive center before, there is another opportunity on the return trip. The parking area is about 0.1 mile farther.

49. Cheesequake Salt Marsh

Type: Dayhike
Difficulty: Easy for children
Distance: 1.5 miles, round trip
Elevation gain: Negligible
Hikable: Year-round
Hours: Dawn to dusk
Information: Cheesequake State Park, Matawan 07747; (732) 566-2161
Admission: Free; fee for parking Memorial Day through Labor Day and for camping

Hiking through Cheesequake State Park is great any time, but in the spring, when the pink lady's slipper are in bloom, it's exceptional. Besides boasting the largest display of lady's slipper in the state, the park offers wood anemone, Jack-in-the-pulpit, trailing arbutus, and other wildflowers. A wildflower identification book is usually a hit with children who enjoy flowers.

About a third of Cheesequake is salt marsh, but don't worry about getting your feet wet. Boardwalks cross over swampy areas such as Hooks Creek, which is a good place to spot muskrats, herons, and ducks. In this area, children can watch fishermen catching blue crabs while you absorb the beauty of the low-growing salt hay and marsh grasses.

Start out early in the day so that you can visit the park's interpretive center, where an informative audio-visual program is presented along with numerous displays.

See driving directions for Hike 48.

The wide, sandy road located next to the trail map leads into the woods. At 0.1 mile, turn left at the sign for the red trail, and proceed across a short boardwalk over a narrow brook. After a gradual uphill stretch, you'll come to the interpretive center. Stop for a visit or continue following the red blazes. The trail dips slightly, then crosses two boardwalks beneath oaks and maples, where you'll probably hear birds chattering. Shortly, you'll reach a long wooden staircase. Counting the steps is a fun game for kids.

After the climb, turn right at the double blue blaze, continuing along a meandering, narrow trail that levels a bit before descending slightly. A salt marsh is to the right. The dominant grasses in this area

Watching swaying, feathery plumes of phragmites is one of the joys along this trail.

include salt hay, which sports 2-foot-high blades that form a dense carpet, and cord grass, which grows in thick clumps about 10 feet high. These grasses provide excellent cover not only for nesting and feeding birds, such as snowy egrets and herons, but also for muskrats, crabs, and diamondback terrapins, which come in from the sea to lay their eggs in the marsh's sand. Twice a day tides wash over the marsh, delivering necessary nutrients to its inhabitants.

Use caution as you make your way to the salt marsh. The long, steep descent at 0.5 mile can be slippery. Grabbing hold of nearby tree trunks helps. You're now on the blue-blazed trail, which heads down to a boardwalk in a few yards. When crossing the wooden bridge, look up to get an idea of the climb that awaits you. The salt marsh is several feet below the surrounding drier areas, where trees and grasses grow. Climbing up from marsh level requires a balancing act, but after the first few steps, the going gets easier. (Wooden stairways will eventually be installed at the fringes of the marsh.) The trail descends briefly after a level area. Head toward the next long boardwalk. Viewing the tall, swaying, feathery plumes of the surrounding phragmites is a joy, especially when the sun is behind them.

When the boardwalk ends, climb the short hill leading immediately into the open. Turn right into the woods at 0.7 mile and in a few yards, head downhill, past stands of mountain laurel. This lovely area is followed by still another boardwalk, and if you're here late in the day, you'll probably see hundreds of birds in the open field.

Turn right at the T on the soft sand road. Just ahead in the open is what locals refer to as the crabbing bridge, the bridge across Hooks Creek. During dry conditions in the summer months, there may not be any water. Stand still and be patient; you'll probably be rewarded by the sight of hermit crabs scurrying around in the mud below, while up ahead, fishermen may be lifting their wire baskets checking for blue crabs.

When you're ready, continue onto the wide, sandy trail ahead. This leads to an open field, a lake, a beach, and a bathhouse. You might want to stop here for a swim.

Cross the dam at about 1 mile and turn right, keeping to the edge of the woods. Pitch pines, identifiable by their bundles of three needles, are dominant in this sandy soil. With the lake to the left, continue on the wide, level trail, climb the staircase, and bear left onto the yellow-blazed trail. Proceed on this narrow path along the edge of the lake, which levels out after a series of ups and downs. Walking slightly uphill again, watch for toads among the rotted logs.

Near a bench the trail turns right sharply. During spring, you'll find a profusion of pink lady's slippers on both sides of the trail. Blueberries, which have drooping white bell-shaped flowers in June, ripen in July and early August—but make certain that they *are* blueberries before you taste them. Continue on the level trail back to the parking area.

Rabbits are a common sight on or off the trail.

50. Poricy

Type: Dayhike
Difficulty: Easy for children
Distance: 1.7 miles, round trip
Elevation gain: Negligible
Hikable: Year-round
Hours: Nature center: summer, Mon.–Fri., 9:00 A.M.–1:00 P.M.; Sun. 12:30–3:30 P.M.; after Labor Day, Mon.–Fri., 9:00 A.M.–4:00 P.M.; Sun. 12:30–3:30 P.M.; trail, daily, dawn to dusk
Information: Poricy Park, P.O. Box 36, Middletown 07748; (732) 842-5966
Admission: Free

This easy hike is perfect for children who are being introduced to hiking. You'll meander in Poricy Park's marsh and deep woods, pass a pond teeming with wildlife, and tramp through a field that's bursting with wildflowers during spring and summer. Children will also enjoy seeing soaring hawks, plump woodchucks, a farmhouse and barn dating back to colonial times, and the visitor center, which features fossils found in the area, an active beehive, and several "hands-on" exhibits.

Pack a shovel, strainer, towel, and change of clothing in the car trunk, and at the end of the hike, surprise them by driving a few minutes to Poricy Brook, where they can dig for fossils in a bed dating back 65 million years. Occasionally, the remains of duckbilled dinosaurs have been found preserved in the green sand and clay, but more common finds are the bivalves—animals with hinged double shells, one dome-shaped and the other flat. Shark's teeth, snails, sea urchins, and sponges have also been found. Park officials say that the best way to find fossils is to sift the sand and gravel in the streambed or search for loose fossils along the banks. Refrain from digging in the banks because this causes erosion. Feel free to take home the best specimens you find.

It's believed that this area was shallow ocean during the Cretaceous period, approximately 65 million to 135 million years ago. Poricy Brook, estimated to be 72 million years old, is part of the sea layer that finally receded. As the water receded, ocean animals died and sank to the bottom, where their bones, teeth, and shells were buried. The cutting action of the brook helps expose those fossils you'll discover.

From the Garden State Parkway, take Exit 114 and go west on Red Hill Road toward Middletown. Turn right on Bamm Hollow Road, which becomes Oak Hill Road. Park at the Poricy Park Nature Center, to the right off Oak Hill Road.

From the center, walk straight past the barn along the Habitat Trail. Joseph Murray, a Scotch-Irish immigrant who enlisted in the Monmouth Militia during the Revolutionary War, built the barn and nearby farmhouse. He was murdered here in 1780, but his family owned the land until 1861. In 1969 the Poricy Park Citizens Committee was formed in an effort to save 250 acres of open space threatened by development. The group donated the land to the township so that everyone could enjoy the outdoors.

Shortly after crossing a small brook, turn right (at 0.3 mile) onto a wide, grassy path. To your right is a ravine where skunk cabbage thrives in spring. Stay to the right. At 0.5 mile, a beautiful view of Poricy Brook appears. In spring, the surrounding apple trees are adorned with pink blossoms, and the tall tulip trees provide a natural umbrella to ward off the sun. The wooden staircase a short distance ahead leads down to the water's edge, an excellent spot to enjoy the flowing stream.

If you look around, you may find tracks of the birds and animals who stop here for a drink. This is also a wonderful spot to search for wildflowers and ferns. In a few yards, you'll reach a dead end; climb

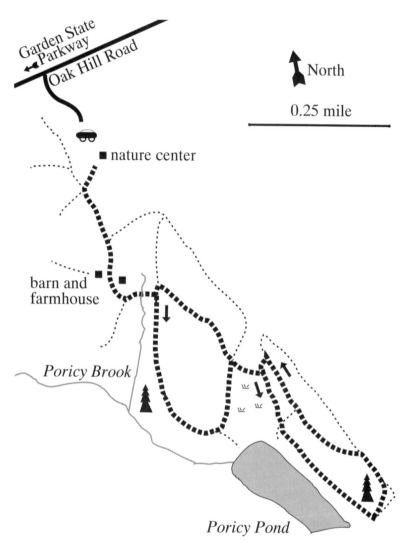

Garden State Parkway

Oak Hill Road

North

0.25 mile

■ nature center

barn and
farmhouse

Poricy Brook

Poricy Pond

back up the steps to where you were and bear right onto the open
lawn area. The ravine will again be on the right. Look for a huge tree
at about 0.8 mile and take another wooden staircase down to the
brook. A boardwalk crosses the swampy area and is flanked on both
sides by skunk cabbage. You'll climb up more steps before turning
right following the edge of the pond. At the end of the trail at about
1 mile, turn left, and at the fork bear left again, continuing along the
railroad tracks. Make another left at the sign to Poricy Park and follow

a level path. Look for the staircase leading to the marsh area at about 1.3 miles. If you're here on a sunny day, you may see a turtle sunning on a rock or a garter snake darting out of the marsh grass. Concentrate on the water for a while; you can often spot frogs, tadpoles, or insects. Bear slightly right after you've climbed up the staircase on the opposite side, walking slightly uphill and straight for about 0.25 mile. Bear right when you see the nature center and proceed to the parking lot.

51. The Hook

Type:	Dayhike
Difficulty:	Easy for children
Distance:	3.6 miles, round trip
Elevation gain:	Negligible
Hikable:	Year-round
Hours:	Dawn to dusk
Information:	Gateway National Recreation Area Park Headquarters, P.O. Box 530, Highlands 07732; (732) 872-0115
Admission:	Beach parking fee

Sandy Hook, part of Gateway National Recreation Area, is a mixture of natural and historic wonders. While breathing in fresh, salt air at "the hook," you'll see dozens of fishing boats and freighters and hear buoys echoing mournful sounds in the distance.

There's more, too. Take along a bag for the treasures washed ashore. After a storm, you may find an old bucket, a twisted tree limb, a fishing net, or an unusual bottle. There are always hundreds of shells on the sand, but caution children to be certain those collected aren't still inhabited. Common shells include those of the quahog clam, which was used by the Lenape Indians for making wampum; the large "house" of the whelk snail; and the discarded shell of the horseshoe crab, which resembles a perfect horseshoe when turned over. Shells with holes in the lower part are known as jingle shells; strung together, they make a dandy wind chime.

Ghosts of the past arise on this hike as well. Although calm today, the hook wasn't always peaceful. Between 1839 and 1848, shipwrecks were so common that Congress had to appropriate funds to build a lifesaving station, one of the first on the Eastern Seaboard. The oldest operating lighthouse in the country can be seen on the hike, which ends past a section of Fort Hancock. The crumbling concrete bunkers and gun emplacements of the fort, built in the 1890s to protect New York Harbor from possible attack, stand today as a reminder of days long gone. While miles of beach are available for exploration, this hike goes to the hook of Sandy Hook, east of Battery Gunnison, which is frequented by nudists during summer months.

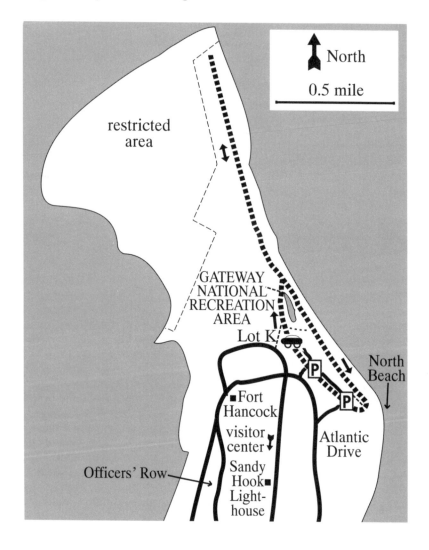

Treasures lie at your feet along the way to "the hook."

Stop in first at the Spermaceti Cove Visitor Center for a 10-minute orientation slide show describing the history of the area. If you want to limber up, try the 1.0-mile circular trail, just outside the building; it passes by one of the largest stands of American hollies on the Eastern Seaboard.

From Atlantic Highlands take NJ-36 east and follow signs to Sandy Hook. The main park road leads past the visitor center to Fort Hancock. Turn right on Atlantic Drive and park in parking lot K, being careful to avoid the potholes.

Start walking the paved road from the north end of parking lot K, following the fence and the old gun battery marked "Battery Peck." Passing the battery, take the wood chip path on the right leading to the sand dunes. The path will bring you to an observation platform with a panoramic view of New York Harbor and New York City.

Where the trail divides, go straight and climb briefly over to the dunes, where you'll have a good view of the long, narrow pond below and the ocean in front of you.

Walk down to the pond, turn left, and as you trudge along the flat sandy trail, you'll see muskrat lodges built along the edge of the pond, and phragmites. Indians used the oozing sap contained in stalks for chewing gum. In about 0.25 mile, the pond is obscured by the thick reeds, and more dunes appear at 0.4 mile. Look for an opening in the chain-link fence and continue to the beach. At the water, bear left (north) toward the hook, but allow time for frequent stops; it's hard to resist stooping to examine the shells and starfish washed up by the tide or admiring the sandpipers that constantly skip along from wave to wave. The tip of the hook is reached at 1.3 miles; the area ahead is restricted.

Retrace your footsteps, continuing past the fence opening through which you entered the beach. To the right, at about 2 miles, stands the 103-foot-tall lighthouse. This National Historic Landmark, built in 1762 to protect ships sailing into New York Harbor, has a 45,000-candlepower electric light that is visible for about 20 miles. Once in a while you may have to duck when hundreds of seagulls fly overhead. You'll be safe in another mile when North Beach is reached. Go around the fence, heading west toward the parking lot exit. From here, with the lighthouse ahead to the left, you'll see a few of the houses in "Officers' Row," the quarters for married officers who commanded the troops manning the fort in the late 1800s. After turning right in the beach parking lot, you'll be able to spot your car in the distance.

---

52. Huber Woods

Type:	Dayhike
Difficulty:	Easy for children
Distance:	2 miles, round trip
Elevation gain:	Negligible
Hikable:	Year-round
Hours:	Trails, daily, dawn to dusk; activity center, Mon.–Fri., 9:00 A.M.–4:00 P.M., except holidays
Information:	Huber Woods Park, c/o Monmouth County Park System, 25 Brown's Dock Road, Middletown 07738; (732) 872-2670
Admission:	Free

Head to the Huber Woods if you only have a couple of hours to spare and want easy hiking in pleasant surroundings. The gradual ups and downs along the trail aren't too taxing and offer a great opportunity to teach children tree identification while meandering through a hardwood forest of oak, tulip, beech, and poplar.

The 256-acre park, donated by the Hans Huber family in 1974, overlooks the Navesink River. In addition to the picturesque farm complex, the German-Swiss–style manor house is currently used for environmental education, displays, nature programs, and cross-country ski clinics.

Drive east from Keyport on NJ-36, exit at the sign for Navesink, and take Grand Avenue, which turns into Navesink Avenue. Pass the Navesink United Methodist Church, make a right turn at the stop sign, and make the first left onto Browns Dock Road. Turn left at the sign

Hikers at the start of the trail cross a vast lawn into the coolness of the woods.

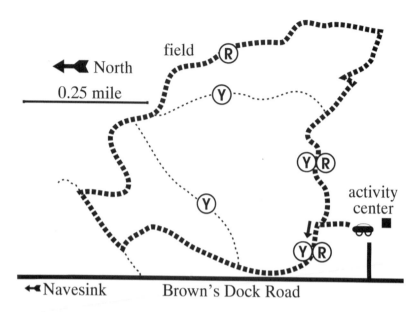

field

← North

0.25 mile

R

Y

Y R

activity
center

Y

Y R

← Navesink   Brown's Dock Road

for Huber Woods, following Brown's Dock Road as it changes from pavement to dirt. Turn left at the sign for the activity center and park nearby.

Walk north (away from the activity center) across the field toward a white sign that indicates the start of the red and yellow trails. If you're here on a hot summer's day, you'll feel the temperature drop as soon as you enter the forest along the narrow, hard-packed sand trail. At the first junction at 0.25 mile, proceed straight on the red trail. This is an excellent area in which to pause and study a few of the interesting plants and creatures found on tree bark. Using a magnifying glass, children can find slow-growing lichens that live on the bark but gain their nourishment from dust and water in the air; larvae of various moth species that may, on first glance, look like twigs; or mealy bugs, which resemble fluffs of wool. They might also discover a spider patiently waiting for an unsuspecting victim.

Continuing along some short sections of soft sand, you'll pass lovely stands of mountain laurel and sassafras. At 0.5 mile, bear right at a T; a gully will be on your right. Make another right at the next junction. Check out the grassy field for grazing horses on the left at 0.75 mile. Large masses of club moss can be found on either side of the trail a bit farther. At the intersection with the yellow trail at just under 1 mile, bear left, following the red markings.

In about another 0.25 mile, you'll enter a grove with impressive Norway spruce where it's so dark you'd swear it was evening. The few houses that appear to the left do not detract from the surrounding beauty. Keep an eye on the blazes as the trail makes several turns. After another 15 minutes or so, the yellow trail joins in from the right on the way back to the field you originally crossed, and leads to the parking area.

53. Clay Court

Type:	Dayhike
Difficulty:	Moderate for children
Distance:	2.2 miles, round trip
Elevation gain:	200 feet
Hikable:	Year-round
Hours:	Dawn to dusk
Information:	Monmouth County Park System, Newman Springs Road, Lincroft 07738; (732) 842-4000
Admission:	Free

Families hiking the Hartshorne Woods for the first time are usually surprised by its steep overlooks and sloping valleys. Three trails, covering a distance of 6 miles, are situated in a dry, upland forest in the heart of New Jersey's coastal plain. In 1975, this 475-acre wilderness tract was purchased by the Monmouth County Park System for use as an undeveloped area. It was named in honor of Richard Hartshorne, who had acquired it from the Lenape Indians for only thirteen shillings.

Wildlife abounds; if you hear a series of loud, sharp noises, it's probably an osprey. Known as a "fish hawk" because of the way it plunges feet first into the water for a meal, the osprey has an impressive 4- to 6-foot wingspan, a brown body, and a broad black cheek patch across its white face. Because children usually concentrate on things at ground level, there's a good chance they'll spot one of the resident raccoons, opossum, or white-tailed deer. The woods also contain a variety of trees, including oak, maple, tulip, and immature chestnuts.

Drive east past Keyport on NJ-36 to a sign for Red Bank Scenic Road, and turn right onto Navesink Avenue. The parking lot is on the left side of the road.

Families are surprised by the steep overlooks, sloping valleys, and wonderful views when hiking the Hartshorne Woods.

There is a large map located next to the parking area at the start of the trails. It's easy to veer off the trail because there are many turns and the markers are not only tiny, but often placed up high on the

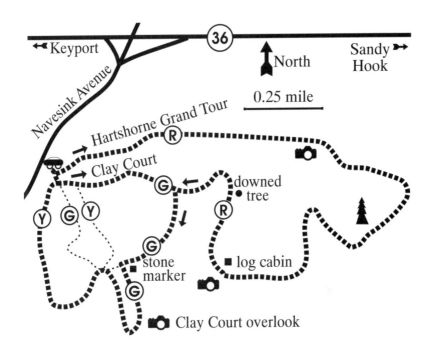

trees. Always backtrack if you've gone for a distance without seeing a blaze.

Following the green blazes, walk uphill. Erosion has made this sandy trail uneven in spots and the loose rocks sometimes give way underfoot. After another short climb, take the left fork where the trail splits, and continue uphill past huge stands of rhododendron and mountain laurel. The path soon levels and leads through mature woods. Just past a small stone marker reading "1875," supposedly for a former estate on these grounds, turn left at a sign pointing to the Clay Court overlook. (The sign is slightly to the left of the trail.) This level trail leads to an impressive view of the Navesink River. The best view is in late fall and winter, when the leaves have fallen. Oaks, profuse in this area, drop hundreds of acorn shells onto the ground below. During spring, numerous species of waterfowl and raptors raise their young in the park. The proximity of the waterways, along with an abundance of fish in the shallow waters, makes this one of their favorite areas.

Carefully descend at a spot marked by a green blaze; the trail is extremely steep and little ones should be held tightly because it's easy to fall on loose, exposed rocks. In a short distance, you'll be ascending steeply; at the top, yellow blazes join in. Stay left on the yellow trail that goes downhill after a short, level stretch. After several short ups and downs, the yellow trail leads back to the starting point.

54. Hartshorne Grand Tour

Type: Dayhike
Difficulty: Easy for children
Distance: 3 miles, round trip
Elevation gain: 200 feet
Hikable: Year-round
Hours: Dawn to dusk
Information: Monmouth County Park System, Newman Springs Road, Lincroft 07738; (732) 842-4000
Admission: Free

Poet Joyce Kilmer, who wrote about his love for trees, would probably have felt at home in the Hartshorne Woods. He'd have appeciated the enormous variety of trees stretching their limbs toward the sky, including a tall tulip tree that sprouted from a downed tree at the end of the trail. The huge stands of mountain laurel and holly, an abundance of common forest mammals, and numerous song and game birds make this a wonderful place to hike during any season. You'll also find many American chestnut saplings here, which is heartening because mature chestnuts throughout the country have been killed by a fungus. It is hoped that this species, once prized by the lumber industry for its wood and by others for its tasty nuts, can survive to maturity.

Drive east from Keyport on NJ-36 to the sign for Red Bank Scenic Road and turn right onto Navesink Avenue. The parking lot is on the left side of the road.

Turn left onto the red trail that starts just behind the trail map near the parking area. Head uphill along the wide, sandy trail. Oak and hickory dominate in this area, but you'll also find sassafras and ironwood. The trail levels out in about 0.25 mile before climbing gradually past old stands of mountain laurel. Watch for the Navesink River off to the right at about 1 mile. Then turn right; as you descend again, you'll be going into the heart of the woods. The trail soon makes another right turn.

The beauty of the pines in this section is overwhelming. Pause and look around; vines appear to be strangling many of the younger trees as they steadily climb up the trunks of the older ones.

As the trail levels out, there's a dramatic change in the composition of the forest: The pines have been superseded by the American holly, which can be as small as a shrub or as big as 50 feet tall and has leathery, spiny-tipped leaves. In winter and early spring, catbirds and mockingbirds munch on the pretty red berries of the female tree.

Slow down as you walk past holly trees at about 1.6 miles so you don't miss an unusual sight: a tulip tree with part of its trunk curving over the trail and the rest rising like a Greek column. Immediately after it is a grand holly tree. Just before you get into the birch tree area, you'll cross an interesting bridge made of sliced tree trunks. The river comes into view once again at 1.75 miles, but an even better view is from a log cabin just ahead. The cabin is used for overnight group camping; reservations are necessary. Whether you camp or not you can still enjoy the surroundings.

From here, the trail levels off before dropping slightly once again. At about 2 miles pretty beeches flourish, recognizable by clear, smooth, light gray bark and 3- to 6-inch-long, sharp-toothed leaves. If you come during winter, look closely at the thin, pointed buds; Thoreau referred to them as "the spearheads of Spring."

In a short distance, mountain laurel covers the hillside, and just after it is the highlight of the hike—a tulip tree growing out from a tree that fell directly over the trail. Kids can't resist walking across this natural bridge, a great spot for taking family photos. When finished, continue on and turn left, following the red blazes. Follow the trail as it steeply descends and leads back to the parking lot.

A hiker rests upon a downed tulip tree across the trail.

182

55. Holmdel Park

Type:	Dayhike
Difficulty:	Easy for children
Distance:	2.5 miles, round trip
Elevation gain:	120 feet
Hikable:	Year-round
Hours:	Dawn to dusk
Information:	Holmdel Park, Longstreet Road, Holmdel 07733; (732) 946-2669 or (732) 842-4000
Admission:	Free

To capture the flavor of what the Garden State was like during the nineteenth century, consider stopping at Longstreet Farm before beginning this pleasant, short hike.

Thanks to the Monmouth County Park Commission, the farm and adjoining land were purchased from Mary Longstreet Holmes Duncan— the sixth generation of the Longstreet family—in 1965, preserving a page from the state's agricultural past. The inside of an eighteenth-century cottage-style farmhouse is on display, as well as horses, mules, hogs, sheep, Jersey milk cows, and other farm animals. Costumed interpreters work the farm as it was worked a century ago.

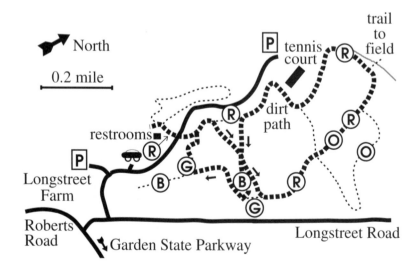

The information booth at the trailhead

Along with the trails, a 9-acre living-history farm and an impressive arboretum make up Holmdel Park—a 339-acre site nestled in the rolling hills of central suburban Monmouth County. The trails meander over much of the land the Longstreets hiked a century ago. Highlights include magnificent stands of beech trees, easily recognized by their smooth bark and down-sweeping branches. Unfortunately, uncaring hikers who have carved their initials into many of these trees have not only marred their beauty, but left them susceptible to disease.

From Garden State Parkway Exit 114 take Red Hill Road south, turn right on Crawfords Corner Road, left on Roberts Road, then right on Longstreet Road. Go through the park entrance and stay right at the road junction; park in parking lot No. 2.

Start uphill on the gravel road just past the restrooms and head

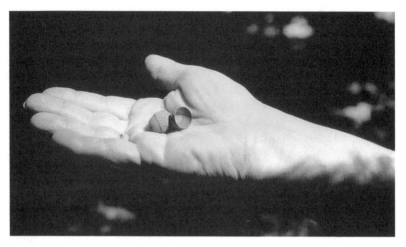

Acorns

toward the tree marked with yellow, green, red, and blue blazes. Stay
with the red trail, crossing the road into the woods. You'll immediately
come to one of the many stations of the fitness trail found throughout
this hike. Be certain to read the directions before doing any of the
exercises.

The sandy trail soon begins a series of gradual ups and downs.
Shortly after going downhill into a ravine, the trail levels. Turn left
at about 0.5 mile. Lovely tulip and oak trees sit atop a hill about 0.2
mile farther, a perfect place for listening to the rustling of leaves on
a windy day. Orange blazes soon join in. As the trail descends, tree
roots seem to sprout up from everywhere. The trail levels again before
beginning another series of ups and downs and makes a left turn at
the bottom of a hill at about 1 mile. In a few yards, you'll climb
gradually once again, heading past beautiful pines. A small brook can
be seen and heard in the ravine to the right. The long wooden bridge
over the brook will take you to an open field. Instead, climb the low
hill ahead and continue walking. A right turn brings you to the tennis
courts. Stay left, hugging the perimeter of the woods, and look for a
dirt path on the left. The trails are poorly marked in this area. Turn
left onto the path, which parallels the auto road for a short distance.
Next, make another left turn, this time following a blue-blazed trail
into the woods, and head gradually downhill. Soon, the green trail
appears. This is one of the prettiest sections of the park. When the
trails split, stay with the green trail, which turns right, climbing
gradually. During spring, the blooms of rhododendron in this area
light up the landscape. Cross the auto road, heading back to the
starting point.

56. Washington Crossing State Park

Type: Dayhike
Difficulty: Easy for children
Distance: 1.3 miles, round trip
Elevation gain: Negligible
Hikable: Year-round
Hours: Trails, dawn to dusk;
nature center, Wed.–Sat.,
9:00 A.M.–4:30 P.M.;
Sun., 11:30 A.M.–4:30 P.M.
Information: Washington Crossing State Park,
355 Washington Crossing-
Pennington Rd., Titusville 08560;
(609) 737-0623
Admission: Free; parking fee from Memorial
Day through Labor Day

Washington Crossing State Park offers ideal trails for first-time hikers, but you'll have to be alert because the route crisscrosses several short trails. While meandering along, it isn't unusual to come face-to-face with a white-tailed deer, especially in early morning or just before sunset. You'll also be able to observe, in different stages of development, a variety of trees, shrubs, and wildflowers. Plan on stopping in at the nature center before or after the hike. Although small, it's crammed with educational "hands-on" exhibits, live turtles, and fish. A naturalist is available to answer any questions.

From the entrance to Washington Crossing State Park on County Route 546, stay right and follow signs to the nature center.

You might want to start by limbering up on the Sensory Trail located next to the nature center. Especially designed for blind persons, this short trail is a good place to feel the staghorn sumac's velvety twigs and to listen to numerous songbirds. The main trails, which begin near the nature center, start at a wide, grassy lawn where natural succession hasn't yet occurred because regular mowing has prevented the usual growth stages.

At the start of the yellow trail, you'll pass a natural area that was used for farming until the 1940s. Since then, nature has reclaimed the land for her own, populating it with a multitude of plants such as broom sedge, a tall grass once used for making brooms, and daisy fleabane, one of the first plants to fill in fields.

Continue going straight, following yellow markers; after crossing

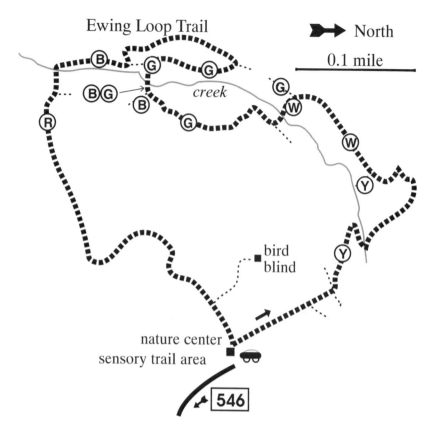

Ewing Loop Trail

North

0.1 mile

creek

bird
blind

nature center
sensory trail area

546

a bridge at 0.2 mile, there's a series of short ups and downs, but for
the most part, the trail is level. Take the white trail at 0.3 mile; then
turn left when the green trail appears at 0.4 mile, but watch out for
the wild roses that will sometimes hook you as you pass by. This area
is a favorite among catbirds, those slate gray, black-capped noisemak-
ers that sound like cats meowing. Soon, you'll reach a creek with lush
growth on both sides. Spicebush, which flowers in March or April,
grows profusely here. Its dried and crushed fruit was used as a lini-
ment. After crossing the creek, turn right, following the green blazes.
A bit farther ahead, bear right at the fork along the green- and blue-
blazed trails. Cross the creek again and bear right onto the green trail.
At about 0.7 mile, bear left onto the Ewing Loop Trail. Cedars abound
here, and cedar waxwings (named for this tree) hang around devour-
ing its fruit. The fragrant, colorful wood of the cedar is prized as a
moth-repellent lining for chests, but for over a century this lightweight
wood was also valued for making pencils. If the ballpoint pen hadn't
been invented, the trees might not exist today.

At 0.8 mile, turn right onto the blue trail; if you're here during spring and summer, you'll smell the sweet aroma of honeysuckle. A beautiful shagbark hickory, which has smoke gray bark and shaggy long strips that seem to be tearing away from the trunk, can be admired at 0.9 mile. Indians used hickory nuts to make a milklike drink, while early pioneers simply cracked the shells open and ate the tasty nuts on the spot.

In a short distance you'll cross the same stream again. Turn right onto the red trail and follow it back to the nature center. Along the way is a path that leads to a bird blind, a good place to get close-up pictures of woodland birds without disturbing them.

Mayapple

57. Herrontown Woods

Type:	Dayhike
Difficulty:	Easy for children
Distance:	1.8 miles, round trip
Elevation gain:	180 feet
Hikable:	Year-round
Hours:	Dawn to dusk
Information:	Mercer County Park Commission, 640 South Broad Street, Trenton 08650; (609) 989-6530
Admission:	Free

Mention Princeton and most people automatically think of the university. Yet, in the heart of this thriving college community, there's a hidden oasis offering easy hiking year-round. Birds are always flying about, and during spring you're guaranteed a bountiful display of bright mountain laurel as well as a variety of colorful wildflowers. Jack-in-the-pulpit, violets, and marsh buttercups are only a few of them.

A joy in any season, Herrontown Woods here offers a challenge: how to cross a narrow stream.

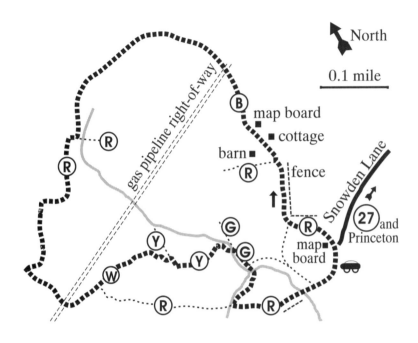

Summer is the ideal season to take advantage of the shade provided by oaks, maples, and beeches, while fall is when Mother Nature paints the leaves bold colors. If you can brave cold weather, plan a visit in the winter, when you can hear ice cracking beneath your feet as you walk along the meandering trails. This is also an easier time to spot the deer.

Sneakers will do, but sturdy shoes are recommended to prevent stubbing toes on the tree roots and rocks.

From NJ-27 just north of Princeton, turn northwest on Snowden Lane. The reservation, on the left, is marked with a sign.

Begin from the right side of the map board located at the eastern end of the parking area, and walk slightly uphill on the narrow, red-blazed trail. A wire fence is on the right. Huge sweet gums, which turn a dazzling crimson in autumn, soon appear. When you reach a clearing with a cottage on the right and a barn on the left, pass between them and take the blue-marked trail. The numerous odd-shaped boulders on and alongside the trail date back to the Triassic period.

At the wide swath of open land at 0.3 mile, cross over the gas pipeline right-of-way, marked by yellow posts, and head back into the woods. The trail, which has been leading gradually uphill, soon levels.

In this area are beautiful beech trees; a few of their golden leaves stubbornly cling to branches through winter, adding a touch of color. In a few yards, mitten-shaped sassafras and ironwood trees follow, and in about 0.5 mile is a stand of tall, shagbark hickory, identified by ragged gray bark curling away from the trunk. This hickory is still valued commercially for smoking meats and for making ax handles.

Turn right onto the red trail at 0.8 mile. As the red trail makes several sharp turns, watch for the blazes; they are sometimes difficult to see against the dark tree trunks.

Cross over the gas pipeline once again at 1.1 miles. The white trail appears shortly. Stay left, following the white markings as the trail descends steeply. Rocks and tree roots in this area are sometimes covered by leaves, so watch your step. Turn right at the junction with the yellow trail, and after crossing the stepping-stone bridge at 1.4 miles, turn right at the T onto the green trail. This short trail ends at a poorly marked junction with the red trail; it can best be recognized as the spot where the green markings disappear. Turn left; a red blaze will eventually come into view and you'll be heading southeast along a boundary fence. After crossing a narrow stream in a few yards, you'll see a grove of pine trees and the parking lot. Deer usually frequent this area.

58. Delaware & Raritan Canal

Type:	Dayhike
Difficulty:	Easy for children
Distance:	4.5 miles
Elevation gain:	None
Hikable:	Year-round
Hours:	Dawn to dusk
Information:	Superintendent, D & R Canal State Park, 625 Canal Road, Somerset 08873; (732) 873-3050
Admission:	Free

For over 150 years, the Delaware & Raritan Canal has been a tribute to the hundreds of laborers who created it. The crews spent countless grueling hours digging the long, deep trench, armed with only picks and shovels. Many died on the job, from the exertion, poor hygiene, and a cholera epidemic. Opened in 1834, this waterway allowed coal barges to move between Philadelphia and New York City.

The canal was closed in 1933 when the train made shipping faster and more economical. Today, it's a major source of drinking water for residences and businesses in twenty-two towns, and since becoming a state park in 1974, it has been used by hikers, canoeists, fishermen, and bicyclists. Trees have sprouted up along the towpath, but in the

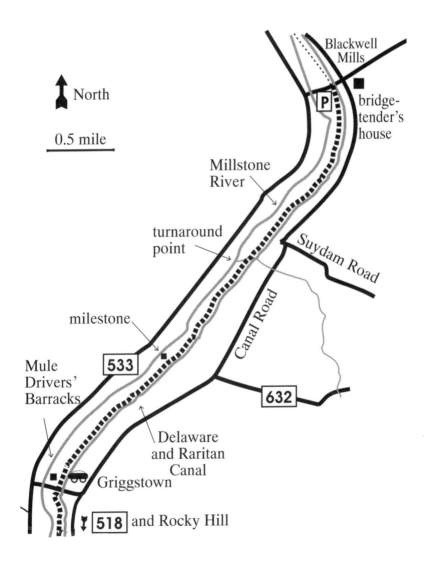

days long gone, when barges plied the water, vegetation was controlled to prevent mule reins from getting tangled.

The hike, through a pretty, secluded area, begins at Griggstown. It can be done either as a round trip or by spotting a second car at Blackwells Mills; the length is nearly the same either way. As you walk along near the water's edge, you'll find thick beds of pickerelweed, identifiable by their elongated, heart-shaped leaves and, from May through October, their showy, blue-flowered spikes. Many hikers carry a hook and line or leave a fishing rod in the car so that they can fish after the hike. Largemouth bass, pickerel, rainbow trout, and catfish can be hooked in this murky water, but you need to have a license.

Although you won't see many houses along this stretch today, stories abound about the old houses with their high wooden picket fences that prevented children from falling into the water. One owner placed empty whiskey bottles on the pickets as a decoration, and much to his surprise, found that passing coal barge crews would aim pieces of coal at the bottles. It didn't take him too long to figure out a way to collect a free supply of coal for the winter!

From Rocky Hill take NJ-518 east for a short distance, and just after crossing the Delaware & Raritan Canal, turn left on Canal Road. At Griggstown, turn left after the canal and park. To spot a second car, continue north on Canal Road, turn left at the T on Suydam Road, and right on Canal Road to Blackwells Mills. Cross the canal and park next to the towpath.

You may wish to visit the Mule Drivers' Barracks in Griggstown before starting the hike. The building, open to the public on Sundays and managed by the historical society, contains old photographs and memorabilia of canal history. Over sixty pivot bridges, fourteen locks with centrally pivoted shutter sluices, an extra lift lock at Lambertville for the narrow feeder canal, guard locks, and aqueducts had to be planned and built.

When ready, walk to the towpath and head north. The buildings on the opposite side of the canal soon disappear, giving way to woods. Surrounded by trees, with the silence broken only by the chirping of birds, the calm water evokes the ambience of a quiet day perhaps a century ago.

As you proceed straight on the wide, packed-dirt trail beneath a canopy of yellow birch, red maple, and tulip trees, be careful not to brush against poison ivy; it not only grows along the entire length of the canal's bank, but also sometimes wraps itself around tree trunks. Poison ivy has three leaves growing from the same point on the stem. In winter, spotting this plant is more difficult. It has white berries and sometimes grows as a furry vine.

Occasionally, a bicyclist will pass by, or you'll see canoeists paddling by. Sometimes, you may hear a "plop-plop" near the bank. Stand quietly for a few seconds and you'll probably spot a frog just before it plunges into the water. On sunny days, turtles bask on the bank or on a log, but no matter which season you come, you'll hear beautiful melodies; over 150 species of birds frequent the area.

At about 1.3 miles, you'll reach a concrete milestone from which the mule team leader could tell the distance to New Brunswick or

While walking along the towpath of the Delaware & Raritan Canal, you can see a variety of trees, birds, canoeists, and a lot more.

Trenton, depending on where the barge was going. The first sign of civilization—a farm—appears on the other side of the canal at a little over 2 miles. In the same area, a pretty brook flows under the canal. This is a convenient spot to turn around, although it is possible to continue for as many miles as desired. If you continue to Blackwells Mills, you'll have an opportunity to see the bridge tender's house, which still stands. The complete history of the canal is described by Elizabeth Menzies in her book *Passage Between Rivers*.

59. Owl Haven

Type:	Dayhike
Difficulty:	Easy for children
Distance:	3 miles, round trip
Elevation gain:	Negligible
Hikable:	Fall and winter are best; tick danger other seasons
Hours:	Trails, dawn to dusk; nature center, Tues.–Sat., 10 A.M.–5 P.M., Sunday 1–5 P.M., or by appointment
Information:	Owl Haven Nature Education Center, 250 Englishtown-Freehold Road, Tennant 07763; (732) 780-7007
Admission:	Free

Owl Haven, located at Monmouth Battlefield State Park, is the newest nature center of the New Jersey Audubon Society. It's also one of the most pleasurable to visit. Stop in at the center before you begin; Director Alice Forshee will allow you to touch live reptiles, amphibians, and her own pet owls. A naturalist for over twenty years, Forshee is licensed by the federal government to rehabilitate injured animals, and can direct you to places along the trail you are most likely to see owls. She'll also show you excellent exhibits of mounted birds, mammal skulls, and tree and seashore specimens common to the area. Ask about the regularly scheduled evening and weekend programs conducted here.

From NJ-9, take the Throckmorton Exit (about 0.75 mile north of NJ-33) and go west on NJ-522 about 1 mile to the entrance to Owl

Haven. The parking lot is just off the road.

Walk along the side of the nature center to the trail sign. Turn left and continue across the cornfield. Deer are common in this area and can be seen during early morning and late afternoon; their tracks usually stand out in the sand. In about 0.25 mile, you'll find a historic trail marker embedded in a stately old black cherry tree at post 2. Turn left here onto the wide, flat, grassy trail that enters the woods. Winged sumac, with its greenish red twigs and leafstalks marked with raised dots, is abundant along this section of trail. Its fruit is arranged in dense red clusters. A lone red cedar stands out opposite post 5, and to the right of the post a poison ivy vine has entwined itself around a tree. Turn right just past the marker. Up ahead are tall, narrow locust trees. A member of the pea family, these trees produce drooping clusters of sweet-smelling, creamy white flowers and 3-inch beans in spring or early summer. A valuable source of timber, they look attractive year-round. The name of the corkscrew-shaped trees found at 0.6 mile remains a mystery to us.

Turn left at the open field a short distance ahead, keeping to the edge of the woods. A large farmhouse will come into view. Stay to the right at the trail junction, and at the T at 0.75 mile, turn right; the woods will be on the left. As you walk along the edge of the cornfield you'll see lots of birds darting in and out of the woods looking for ears of corn to munch on. Continue through the break in the trees into an open area. After crossing the field, the trail follows the edge of

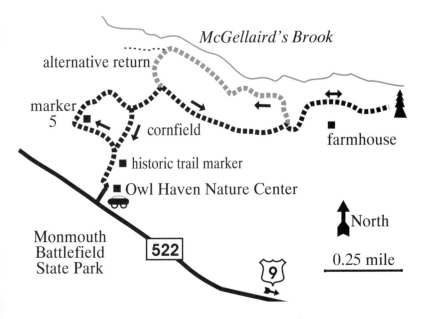

the woods. At the trail junction leading to the barn area, go straight. You'll reach a magnificent beech atop a knoll at 1.5 miles; this remote spot is your destination.

At this point, return the way you came, heading back past the road junction at 1.6 miles. On a recent visit during late fall, we were unable to find the path across the field that we used on the outbound trip. If you have the same problem, or if you want variety, try the following: Stay right at the opening through the trees at 1.9 miles and follow the trail as it hugs the border of the woods, on the right. Tiny McGellaird's Brook is visible through the trees. Wild roses and tall weeds appear as the trail curves. This is an excellent area to spot moles, voles, shrews, and rabbits. We've often heard mating calls of woodcocks here, as well as the sweet songs of other birds, and have seen red-tailed hawks searching for a tasty mouse.

At about 2.3 miles, the woods close in; keep an eye out for a cross trail leading off to the left. Follow this trail, which, though wide here, peters out in a short distance. Continue straight and bushwhack your way through the woods, climbing uphill. At the top, you'll come to the field you came through earlier. Turn right on the wide trail, keeping the trees on your right, and follow it back to the parking area.

Wildflowers abound during spring at Owl Haven.

60. Turkey Swamp

Type:	Dayhike or overnight camping
Difficulty:	Easy for children
Distance:	2.2 miles, round trip
Elevation gain:	Negligible
Hikable:	Year-round; crowded during summer months
Hours:	Dawn to dusk
Information:	Park Ranger, Turkey Swamp Park, Nomoco Road, RD 4, Freehold 07728; (732) 462-7286
Admission:	Free; fee for camping

Heavy rains came down the first day we camped at Turkey Swamp Park. History repeated itself the second day, but we made a wise decision in leaving our dry tent to hike in the rain, because the trails are usually wet anyway. Although the soil is sandy here on the north-

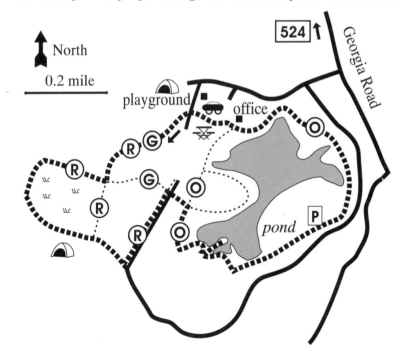

While skirting the lake, you'll see boaters.

ern fringe of the Pine Barrens, the water table lies just beneath the earth's surface, which often makes for swampy conditions; hence the name Turkey Swamp.

Most hikers are disappointed when they don't encounter any turkeys (the park is named for the town of Turkey, now known as Adelphia), but the flat, sandy trails and variety of vegetation—scrub oak, young white oaks, and a thick understory of pepper bush, huckleberries, and blueberries—make up for it. Tall, stately pitch pines are also in evidence, along with stands of sweet gum. The second part of this walk follows the edge of a manmade lake, where canoes and paddleboats may be rented during the summer.

 From US 9, go west on NJ-524 and then left onto Georgia Road to the park entrance. Follow the sand road to the main parking lot.

Start at the office next to the parking area, following the red and green blazes through the picnic area and playground; cross the road and continue on the red trail. At about 0.3 mile, where the green trail turns left and the red trail divides, turn right onto the red trail, which leads into a small bog. The bog area is recognizable by an abundance of grayish green sphagnum moss on the swamp floor. The Indians discovered that sphagnum moss made a terrific natural diaper; it's still prized today by plant nurseries as packing material because it can hold ten times its weight in water. With a magnifying glass, you can find two carnivorous plants, the sundew and pitcher plants, in the moss.

Quench your thirst at the hand pump in the Wilderness Campground area in about 0.5 mile (just past an outhouse). At just under 1 mile, turn left on the road to the open field area; at the green marker past a clump of trees at 1 mile, turn right heading toward the pond. Cross over the short footbridge, turn right again onto the orange trail, and walk across the field. In this area, the orange trail joins part of a fitness trail, going through a wet area with the pond on the left. For an overall view of the pond, leave the trail at about 1.2 miles to walk onto a small peninsula. After returning to the main trail, continue along the perimeter of the woods until a narrow, sandy path appears to the left at about 1.4 miles; this passes near a flooded area with decaying tree trunks.

A short distance ahead is a large open area used for overflow parking on crowded summer days; walk straight ahead to the end, turn left, and pick up the orange trail again. Another sweeping view of the pond comes at 1.7 miles, but the best view is a few yards farther.

Swampy areas often support a profusion of the pink lady's slipper.

When you come out of the woods, follow along the shoreline. Usually lots of geese and ducks can be found on this side of the pond. Pick up the orange blaze again, go to the end, turn left, and continue to the office and parking area. Kids get a special treat at the end of this hike; there's another play area here.

Note: Camping for tents and trailers is available by reservation or on a first-come, first-served basis from March 1 to November 30. The Wilderness Campground area is a favorite of organized youth groups.

61. Manasquan Reservoir Perimeter Trail

Type:	Dayhike
Difficulty:	Moderate for children
Distance:	5 miles, round trip
Elevation gain:	None
Hikable:	Year-round
Hours:	Dawn to dusk
Information:	Monmouth County Park System, Newman Springs Road, Lincroft 07738; (732) 938-6760
Admission:	Free

Fishermen can strike it rich here reeling in bass, trout, and panfish. Sailors with electric motorboats, sailboats, kayaks, and canoes can glide through the water. Bikers can pedal with ease. But hikers are the luckiest of all. They can combine exercise with a close look at a variety of habitats while hiking along the Manasquan Reservoir Perimeter Trail. The land around the New Jersey Water Supply Authority's 720-acre reservoir is wetland, grassy plains, and a hemlock grove.

 From NJ-9 just north of its intersection with I-95, take Georgia Tavern Road east. Turn right on Windeler Road to the entrance, on the left.

Start from the right side of the parking lot as you face the reservoir; the trail goes between two wooden posts. With the water to your left, bear right onto the wide, grassy trail. Cross over the dike, through an area frequented by ducks. At the T in 0.25 mile, turn left onto the gravel road heading toward the water. The trail soon becomes a wide dirt path that goes past junipers, known for their wonderful aroma and their use in cedar closets and chests. These trees can reach a height of 50 feet at maturity. Scattered stands of mountain laurel at 0.6 mile make a colorful appearance each spring, and at 0.8 mile hollies flank both sides of the trail. Even on the dreariest winter's day their red berries add a bright touch of color to the surroundings. If you've come during spring, frogs will be sounding their mating call; if you get too close, they'll leap into the water.

Although the trail sometimes meanders near the roadway, that won't detract from the woodsy atmosphere, especially at the 1-mile mark after you've crossed a bridge into the swampy area. At this point,

Some of the trees along the shoreline of the Manasquan Reservoir stand in water and will eventually die.

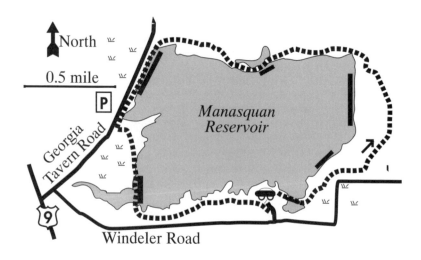

you'll see a large dam across the water, and a bit farther ahead, you will come to a lovely hemlock grove. The trail turns left and away from the road again 0.25 mile later, facing toward the main dam. Every so often, a seagull can be seen flying low over the reservoir, letting out a mournful cry if it hasn't yet found dinner. The trail swings to the water's edge at 1.9 miles, and is almost directly opposite the parking area. Ahead, the contrast is amazing. On the left side is open water; on the other, a stagnant, wet area with trees that were here before the dam was built. Eventually they'll die, but now they make for an eerie sight.

The nearby tall, feathery phragmites indicate wet ground and, according to Peterson's *Field Guide to Edible Wild Plants,* the young stems "can be dried and pounded into a fine powder which, when moistened, is roasted like marshmallows." It's illegal to pick them, but very satisfactory to watch them sway in the slightest breeze.

Without even having to look up you'll know when you've reached the sweet gum trees—you'll be stepping on their large brown seed balls! Turn left before the road. The sound of traffic nearby may be intrusive at this point, but the beauty of the trees standing in water is some consolation.

Continue past the parking lot at 3 miles and cut back, left, into the woods onto a gravel trail. The reservoir is blocked by trees, but reappears at a spot where Canada geese often hang out. Crossing on a narrow dike that separates the marsh from the reservoir, you'll feel as though you're walking on water. The trail goes through some wet spots before entering deep woods. Continue until it intersects the main entrance road. Turn left to return to the parking lot.

Tree trunks stand like soldiers in this continuously flooded area, now a graveyard for trees.

62. Allaire

Type:	Dayhike or overnight camping
Difficulty:	Easy for children
Distance:	3.5 miles, round trip
Elevation gain:	Negligible
Hikable:	Year-round
Hours:	Dawn to dusk
Information:	Allaire State Park, Box 220, Farmingdale 07727; (732) 938-2371
Admission:	Free; fee charged for parking Memorial Day through Labor Day (exept Tuesdays) and for camping

Although you'll be arriving and parking at Allaire Village, save exploring this historic site for after the hike. The village and land James P. Allaire purchased in 1822, along with Howell Furnace, are now managed by the state and are within Allaire State Park. You'll be passing through lush woods beside tiny streams where ninety-four varieties of wildflowers can be seen. For bird lovers, there's always the possibility of spotting a blue-winged warbler, a ruby-throated hummingbird, or dozens of other species. You might even see a prancing woodcock performing his courting ceremony.

Allaire, with only the barest grade-school education, was a man of great vision and talent. At the age of nineteen, he was credited with having built the brass air chamber in Robert Fulton's steamship, the *Clermont*. Later, he turned the Howell Furnace operation into one of the finest bog ironworks in the country. Layers of bog ore and charcoal were dumped into the furnace stack, and the intense heat of the fire turned these ingredients into a molten mass; the resulting chemical action caused the iron to separate and fall to the bottom. The molten iron poured out through another opening and became solid iron. In time, Allaire rebuilt the original village, adding row houses for his 500 workers and their families, as well as shops and a church. It wasn't surprising when people began referring to the entire operation as "Allaire." Unfortunately, when anthracite was discovered in Pennsylvania in 1846, bog iron was no longer in demand and the workers eventually left. Allaire's son stayed on, but after he died in 1901, Arthur Brisbane, a top editor under William Randolph Hearst, bought the land. Upon his death in 1941, Brisbane's widow donated the land to the state.

Campsites in the state park are spacious and shaded, perfect for overnight or a weekend. As a bonus, you might want to board the Pine Creek Railroad, the first operating steam train exhibit in New Jersey and one of the earliest in the United States.

 From the Garden State Parkway, take Exit 98 near Belmar and follow I-195 west to Exit 31B (NJ-524, Allaire Road), then follow signs to Allaire Village.

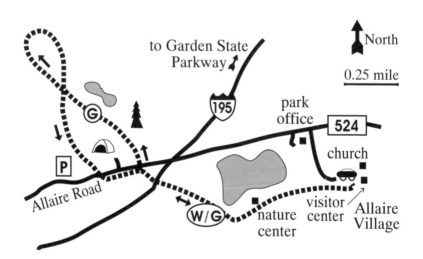

The Episcopal church Allaire built for his community, visible from the parking lot, is unusual in that the steeple was built over the pulpit because the front of the building couldn't support it! Walk toward the row houses and the visitor center, where you'll see a trail sign pointing to the nature center. Follow a white arrow on a green blaze onto a wide, sandy trail next to a small stream, to the right past a picnic grove. At about 0.25 mile, turn right over the wooden bridge if you want to stop at the nature center. Otherwise, continue straight. Here and there are stands of mountain laurel, and at about 0.5 mile is what has become a burial ground for trees in an area that's been flooded repeatedly. Their trunks stand like soldiers guarding the water that surrounds them. I-195 appears overhead briefly at 0.8 mile, but the scenery more than makes up for this intrusion.

Holly

In another 0.1 mile, turn left on Allaire Road walking toward traffic, but exercise caution, as cars come by at high speeds. In a few yards, at a break in the wooden fence on the opposite side of the road, cross over and follow the green blaze. Almost immediately, on the right, is an impressive sycamore, its peeling white bark standing out against a clear blue sky on a winter's day. At 1 mile, a campground appears, and a short distance ahead is another tree graveyard at the edge of a wide expanse of water. This is a pretty spot to sit and wait for deer.

At about 1.6 miles, check out both sides of the trail for impressive holly trees; during winter their red berries add a brilliant splash of color against the snow blanket. The water disappears from view in a few yards, and this area containing pine and oak is usually good for birding. A lovely pine grove is just ahead.

At the crossroad in another 0.2 mile, continue straight, walking southwestward on a narrow, sandy path. Cross through the parking area at 2.5 miles, go left at the arrow, and walk along Allaire Road again, using caution as you walk facing traffic, past the campground entrance. The shoulder is quite wide. Cross the road at the green blaze, continuing the way you came.

63. Shark River Park

Type: Dayhike
Difficulty: Easy for children
Distance: 2.4 miles, round trip
Elevation gain: Negligible
Hikable: Year-round
Hours: 8:00 A.M. to dusk
Information: Shark River Park, Monmouth County Park System, Newman Springs Road, Lincroft 07738; (732) 842-4000
Admission: Free

This pleasant hike can be combined with extra exercise at the fitness stations. You'll pass through several habitats, including a coastal river and floodplain, gravel-capped sandy hills, a cedar swamp, and several sphagnum bogs. Wildflowers are abundant here in spring, but the trail is great any season. Waterproof shoes are recommended because the trail is often wet.

From NJ-33 just east of the Garden State Parkway turn south on Schoolhouse Road. Turn right at the Shark River Park entrance to get to the parking area.

Walk back to the parking entrance, cross the road, and continue straight to the trail marked with red and green blazes. Pitch pine, sporting three needles to a bundle and cones armed with sharp prickles, is dense in this area. Even after shedding their seeds, the empty cones cling stubbornly to the branches for years. The tree is named for that sticky, black pitch oozing out of the buds and branches. As you head downhill, you'll see oaks and mountain laurel, with a thick understory of bracken fern, pepper bush, blueberry, sheep laurel, and catbrier.

After crossing a wooden bridge over a small brook, walk uphill and turn left at 0.1 mile, following the green blazes. The trail reaches a long wooden staircase leading down to a narrow, meandering, sandy path along the bank of the Shark River. Climb the steep stairs at nearly 0.5 mile and, after climbing another staircase, return to the riverbank. In a few yards, after ducking under some overhanging vines, you'll cross a short boardwalk and stairs. Check the trail carefully just after this point: It makes an immediate right turn away from the river but then returns again in a short distance.

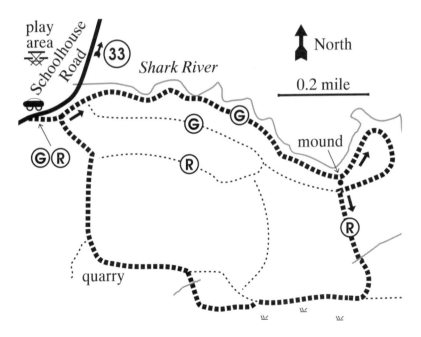

At 0.75 mile, follow the staircase uphill and continue winding left; the trail levels before veering away from the bank, descends gradually, and levels again in another 0.25 mile when the river reappears. Bear right; the water will be in sight on the left. A group of buildings mars the view to the left, but you'll quickly reach the river's bank and then head away from the water for the last time. Civilization is left completely behind once you reach the steps and head southwest along a wide, level trail through the forest. Watch for a mound of soil on the right in another 0.2 mile and turn left onto the unmarked red

The narrow, meandering Shark River

trail. (If you reach a red blaze along the main trail, you've gone too far.) A series of steps leads down to a bog, an excellent area to pause and search for insect-eating sundew and pitcher plants, as well as frogs and turtles. After crossing this section, you'll be surrounded by an impressive 12-foot-high stand of mountain laurel.

After crossing a brook, continue uphill to a long boardwalk and a staircase that leads to a large, grassy field. Turn right immediately, and in a few feet, turn right again into the woods. Steps gradually descend to a T; turn right here, heading west. This raised trail cuts through a cedar swamp. At the Y, bear left onto a grassy trail, which often is muddy after heavy rains or winter melts. You'll be crossing, via a boardwalk, over a lovely stream at 1.7 miles; at the T, turn left onto the sandy road. If you're feeling energetic, practice a few situps and leg raises at one of the fitness stops, or walk straight ahead to the abandoned quarry at 1.9 miles. At the T turn right into the woods. After reaching the sand road at fitness stop 27 (just before the traffic road), turn left following the red trail. Watch out for exposed tree roots on the way back to the parking lot.

The play area, open from 8:00 A.M. to 5:00 P.M., is perfect for a cool-down period.

---

64. Rancocas Woods

Type:	Dayhike
Difficulty:	Easy for children
Distance:	1.4 miles, round trip
Elevation gain:	Negligible
Hikable:	Year-round
Hours:	Trails, daily, dawn to dusk; nature center, Tues.–Sun., 9:00 A.M.–5:00 P.M.
Information:	Rancocas Nature Center, 794 Rancocas Road, Mount Holly 08060; (609) 261-2495
Admission:	Free; donation accepted

When the temperature plummets, the Rancocas Nature Center is the perfect place to plan a short, brisk hike—one guaranteed to warm the body as well as the spirit. Before heading for the trail, visit the

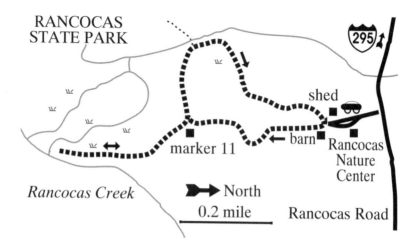

RANCOCAS STATE PARK

shed

marker 11 ← barn Rancocas Nature Center

Rancocas Creek

▶▶ North
0.2 mile

Rancocas Road

nature center. Housed in a century-old house bordered on both sides by Rancocas State Park, the center—operated by the New Jersey Audubon Society—has an extensive reference library and boasts numerous "please-touch" exhibits of the flora and fauna of the area.

If you don't want to brave cold weather, come another time of year. Deer can usually be spotted in the huge open field, especially around sunset, and you'll find a variety of habitats where over 200 plants and about 100 species of birds have been found. You'll also see Rancocas Creek, an excellent array of trees, and the 183-foot "mount" that the town of Mount Holly was named for.

From I-295 Exit 44A in Rancocas, head east on Rancocas Road about 1.8 miles to the nature center entrance on the right.

From the parking lot, begin on the flat, grassy trail going toward the field. You're bound to spot meadow voles, cottontail rabbits, woodchucks, ringneck pheasants, or bobwhites. In about 0.1 mile, looking east (left) over the tree line, is a 183-foot-high ridge of sand and gravel. This is all that remains from when south Jersey was submerged under the ocean about 100 million years ago. During summer months, tall grasses called "reed canary grass" can be found just ahead; this is one of our few native field grasses, and one of the thirty different grasses found along the trails. Look down while hiking through the dense stand of pine at around 0.2 mile and you'll probably find dozens of deer tracks. A few yards farther is a group of European larches; these pines are distinguised by needles growing on short spur branches in clusters of a dozen or more. Unlike most conifers, this particular species sheds its needles during winter, thereby reducing water loss when the soil freezes.

In another 0.25 mile are handsome black locust trees, identifiable

A lunch break next to Rancocas Creek is perfect.

by compound leaves and thorny twigs. Introduced from the South, they were planted in Colonial days chiefly as a supply of rot-resistant wood for making fence posts. Each May, they bloom with white, pealike flowers. When you reach an old woods road, indicated by marker No. 11 and a blue dot, turn left. Although this trail is often quite wet, it's worth the short detour to see Rancocas Creek. While going downhill, you'll pass by old hollies and, in the wetter area, umbrella magnolia and sour gum. The thickets surrounding the water's edge are loaded with fragrant spicebush, sweet pepper bush, and arrowwood.

When you're ready, return to the main trail and turn left. Before the 1-mile point, you'll see a huge "buttonwood" or, as it's commonly known, a sycamore. If you look closely, you'll find a hollow place in the stub of a branch jutting over the trail that serves as home for raccoons and sometimes gray squirrels. Woodpeckers are usually hard at work drilling for tiny insects.

As you meander toward a short boardwalk laid over a swampy area, note the abundance of fern and Queen Anne's lace. Red cedars, one of the first trees to invade abandoned fields, appear about 0.25 mile before the trail returns to the starting point.

65. Deep Hollow

Type: Dayhike
Difficulty: Moderate for children
Distance: 6.3 miles, round trip
Elevation gain: Negligible
Hikable: Year-round
Hours: Dawn to dusk
Information: Lebanon State Forest,
P.O. Box 215, New Lisbon 08064;
(609) 726-1191
Admission: Free

Don't drive too fast or you may miss the beginning of the trailhead, located in the tiny town of Ong's Hat. A mere pinhead on the map, Ong's Hat consists of a market and family restaurant. In the 1840s, however, it was widely known for its cranberry cultivation.

The town was supposedly named for Jacob Ong, a robust Pennsylvania Quaker who loved to drink and dance. Ong ran a tavern in the 1700s and one night, when he might have had one drink too many, he tossed his hat high up onto the limb of an oak tree. Too high to retrieve, the hat became a conversation piece. Customers would yell to newcomers, "There's Ong's Hat." By 1828, it seemed only natural to adopt this cry officially as the town's name.

Ong's Hat is the northern terminus of the Batona Trail, a 50-mile-long pink-blazed path through the pinelands of southern New Jersey that was charted and built by the Batona Hiking Club of Philadelphia in 1961. The trail was designed to offer a true wilderness experience, despite the fact that it cuts across several roads and is accessible by car at a number of points. It passes through some of the most scenic areas of the "pine barrens," a section of the state noted for its unusual plants, including several insect-eating species.

From the junction of routes 72 and 70 at Four Mile circle (about 10 miles southeast of Mount Holly), take Buddtown Road north about 1.7 miles to Ong's Hat and turn right on a small road marked by pink blazes to a parking lot.

The pink blazes of the Batona Trail lead back to the main road and then indicate left turns into the woods. At the beginning, you'll be walking under tall, thin pitch pines. Although the trunks have been charred by repeated fires, this hearty tree always springs back to life again. Scattered about are luscious blueberries and huckleberries, but

Taking a rest break in the heart of the Pine Barrens

you'll have lots of competition if you want to grab a handful because the woods are teeming with wildlife.

Use caution when crossing the sand roads, although they're usu- ally not busy. The first of these is encountered at about 0.25 mile. Turn right at the next sand road, then right again back into the woods, making a left almost immediately at the double blaze. Pine is the dominant tree here, with an occasional oak, until about 0.6 mile when

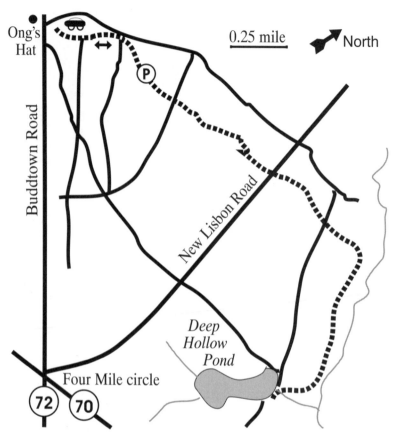

Ong's Hat

Buddtown Road

0.25 mile

North

New Lisbon Road

Deep Hollow Pond

Four Mile circle

72 70

the oak becomes more profuse. Stands of mountain laurel burst into a spectacular display during spring. As the trail narrows, pines take over again. Another sand road crosses the trail at about 1 mile.

From this point, the trail meanders in and out of a mixed pine and oak forest, and the only sound is the cry of a bird or an occasional plane. Use caution when crossing paved New Lisbon Road at 1.4 miles and a wide sand road 0.4 mile later. The trail descends gradually at 2 miles and is flanked on both sides by mountain laurel. If you've come in July or August, you'll also find wintergreen sporting brilliant red berries. From here, you'll be walking along a ridge with slight ups and downs for about a mile. A gully will be to the left and a hill to the right. As you approach Deep Hollow Pond at about 3 miles, watch for cars along the blacktop road. If there aren't too many insects, the beach makes a nice spot to take a break. Bullfrogs usually monopolize the pond in spring, when their bellowing mating call can be heard. Return to the parking area the way you came.

66. Pakim Pond

Type: Dayhike
Difficulty: Moderate for children
Distance: 6.5 miles, round trip
Elevation gain: Negligible
Hikable: Year-round; summer months crowded and buggy
Hours: Dawn to dusk
Information: Lebanon State Forest, P.O. Box 215, New Lisbon 08064; (609) 726-1191
Admission: Free

Each winter we hike a small section of the 41-mile-long pink-blazed Batona Trail that leads to Pakim Pond, a crown jewel of Lebanon State Forest. If you come in warm weather, pack a bathing suit. The water, stained by iron deposits in the soil, may be the color of dark tea, but it's clean. We love to come during winter when the crowds and insects are gone, and the rich green color of the pines adds warmth on the bleakest day. Pitch pine, named for the sticky sap oozing out from its branches and buds, is the dominant tree because it is extremely fire-resistant. It has reddish bark, sharp, prickled cones, and three needles in each bundle.

Beneath this area lies a huge reservoir believed to contain 17 trillion gallons of clean water. Aboveground, a variety of rare plants, stands of pine, cedar swamps, and over 350 species of birds, reptiles, amphibians, and mammals make this a unique wilderness area.

From the traffic circle (near Pemberton) linking NJ-70 and NJ-72, take NJ-72 south for about 1 mile, turning left at the sign for Lebanon State Forest. Drive to park headquarters and park in the large lot.

After obtaining a nature trail guide of Pakim Pond from park headquarters, turn right (heading south) and look for a sign showing the way to Batona Trail. Follow this short connecting trail and then turn left onto the pink-blazed Batona Trail toward Pakim Pond. Caution: Several sand roads cross the trail; be certain to check for traffic before crossing.

Walking on a carpet of pine needles over fine, white sand, you'll pass many red oaks mixed in with the pines. In about 1 mile, you'll come to two small hills. Following the well-marked trail, turn left at

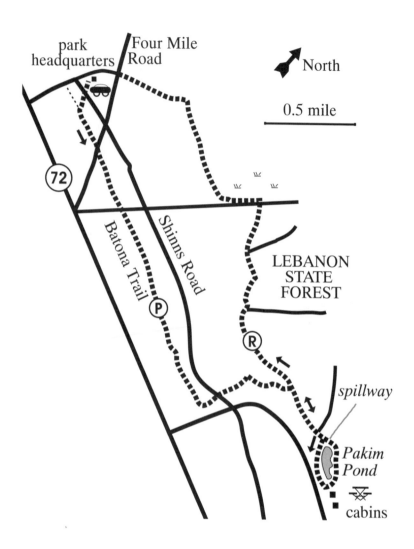

park headquarters

Four Mile Road

North

0.5 mile

72

Batona Trail

Shinns Road

LEBANON STATE FOREST

P

R

spillway

Pakim Pond

cabins

1.9 miles, cross Shinns Road, then turn right at 2.2 miles. Cross over a boardwalk and turn right at 2.5 miles where the trail widens. The next right, at 2.8 miles, will lead to the pond and picnic tables. Pakim Pond, named after the Lenape Indian word for "cranberry," was previously used as a reservoir to store water for flooding a nearby cranberry bog. In the late 1930s, it was developed as a swimming and picnic area.

This is a good place to stop for lunch. In late fall or winter, take your choice of the delightful picnic spots, where you can observe the reflections of the evergreens in the brownish water. Although swimming is nice during warm weather, it can get quite crowded here, especially on weekends.

After sharing lunch with friends on a chilly winter day, we circled the pond in a counterclockwise direction, beginning with a narrow trail grown in with mountain laurels. Seasonal rental cabins are to the right. Turn left after about 0.25 mile, where the pink blaze reappears, and proceed to the footbridge for a different view of the pond. Then continue on, following the pink blazes.

Where red cedars hug the water's edge, you can find clumps of sphagnum moss and two insect-eating plants, the sundew and pitcher plants. Painted turtles usually bask in the sunshine. Continue to the spillway at 3.5 miles, where fishermen sometimes land catfish and pickerel.

Pakim Pond, the crown jewel of Lebanon State Park

When you arrive back at the picnic area, keep following the pink blazes, which will take you back toward the starting point. In a few yards, turn left at the double pink blaze, but at 3.9 miles, leave the Batona Trail and go straight ahead onto the red-blazed path.

The red trail follows old sand roads and paths through thick woods, and is wide enough for several people to walk abreast. Those long, narrow cigar-shaped pine cones on the forest floor are from pitch pines. At 5 miles, the trail turns left and passes through a cedar swamp for about 0.25 mile before thick stands of pine emerge again. Watch for blazes: The soft white-sand trail makes several turns. Finally, at about 6.4 miles, the red trail ends at a blacktop road. Park headquarters is visible just to the left.

Note: Camping, available at designated places along the Batona Trail, and also in Lebanon Forest and Wharton Forest, is by permit only; contact Lebanon State Forest headquarters for further information.

67. Cattus Island

Type:	Dayhike
Difficulty:	Easy for children
Distance:	2.9 miles, round trip
Elevation gain:	Negligible
Hikable:	Year-round
Hours:	Trail, dawn to dusk; office, daily, 8:30 A.M.–4:30 P.M. except holidays
Information:	Cattus Island Cooper Environmental Center, 1170 Cattus Island Boulevard, Toms River 08753; (732) 270-6960
Admission:	Free

Cattus Island Park is on a peninsula dividing Silver Bay from Barnegat Bay. If you could see it from above, after the tide has flooded the marsh, you'd see why it's called an "island." Originally used by homesteaders for raising livestock and salt hay, and later purchased by New York importer John V. A. Cattus as a private retreat for hunting and fishing, the area was first opened to the public as a county park in 1981.

Salt marshes and wetlands make up 70 percent of the 500-acre salt marsh and pine forest tract, with bullrush, salt hay, cord grass, and common reed the primary salt-tolerant plants. Among the other 300 species are false heather, lady's slipper, turkey beard, pixie, and sand myrtle. White marshmallow makes a brilliant appearance in August, while holly and pine add a touch of color during winter.

From Toms River, take Fischer Boulevard north from NJ-37, turn right on Cattus Island Boulevard, then left into the park.

Stop in at the Cooper Environmental Center upon arrival. The 5,000-square-foot solar energy building houses excellent educational exhibits and affords a close-up look of some of the critters you're likely to meet on the trail. These include the eastern king snake, the most common in the area, and the black rat snake, which, growing up to 9 feet, is one of New Jersey's largest. Frogs, salamanders, and toads, as well as 100-million-year-old fossils found in Monmouth and Ocean counties, add to the enjoyment. A naturalist is always on hand to answer questions.

Turn right from the front of the center building onto a dirt road, pass through the gate or go around it, and continue across the salt marsh. Binoculars come in handy for viewing the birds that usually congregate in this section, which has several small circular trails. To keep directions simple (and minimize chances of getting lost), note that transfers from one trail to another generally involve left turns.

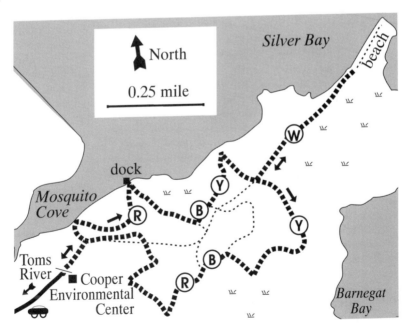

The marsh is an excellent area for spotting Canada geese and other wildlife.

Turn left onto the wide, sandy red trail at 0.2 mile; Mosquito Cove will be on the left as you walk through pine and oak woods. A tiny beach and dock appear at 0.4 mile. In another 0.2 mile, at a T and double red blaze, turn left onto the Blue Trail. Here, with Silver Bay to the left, tall hollies form a living canopy. At a double blue blaze, continue straight ahead onto the yellow trail. In a few yards, after rounding the bend, you'll find cedars along the water's edge. The narrow, meandering trail reaches the white trail, which is a wide path, at about 1 mile; turn left here. Look for deer and birds in the salt marsh on the right. In 0.25 mile is a long strip of beach, a perfect place for lunch or a rest. When you've had your fill of the pleasant sound of water slapping against the shore, turn back through the salt marsh and turn left at the double yellow blaze leading back into the woods at 1.6 miles. The water and holly trees disappear from view as oaks take over on this narrow, winding trail. There are lots of cedars and a pretty view of the marsh at 2 miles. At the T turn left onto the blue trail for a short distance, then left again onto the red trail. In a few yards, you'll be back into pine, oak, and holly woods. After reaching a double red blaze at 2.4 miles, take a short side trip to the left for a fantastic view of open country. Explore this edge of the marsh before returning to the main trail. At the main trail, at 2.7 miles, turn left, heading back to the parking area.

68. Island Beach State Park

Type:	Dayhike
Difficulty:	Easy for children
Distance:	3 miles, round trip
Elevation gain:	Negligible
Hikable:	Year-round
Hours:	Dawn to dusk
Information:	Island Beach State Park, P.O. Box 37, Seaside Park 08752; (732) 793-0506
Admission:	Fee year-round; higher charge in summer

The best time for exploring this barrier island is between Labor Day and Memorial Day. That's when the crowds are gone and parking is plentiful. Binoculars will come in handy for zooming in on a few of the 240 species of birds that frequent the area; among them are three on the endangered list—the black skimmer, least tern, and piping plover. You'll feel the salt spray from the waves breaking onshore, and the hike will lead you to a fine view of the Barnegat Lighthouse, which was built in 1858. Bring along a bag for collecting shells and other small treasures tossed up by the waves.

To learn more about the fauna and flora of Island Beach, make your first stop the Aeolium, 1.5 miles from the entrance gate (open weekends, 9:00 A.M. to 4:00 P.M.). Here, you can view slide shows, browse through numerous "hands-on" exhibits, and, just outside the building, limber up on the excellent 0.13-mile-long nature trail. Identified on this short trail are the prickly pear, aglow in June with brilliant yellow flowers and in autumn with bright red fruit; a dwarf red cedar forest; bayberry shrubs, a favorite source of food for migrating myrtle war-

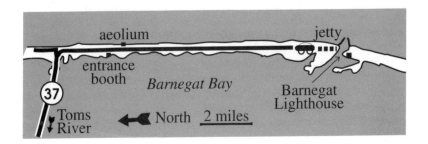

blers, as well as the source of wax for fragrant bayberry candles; and the shadbush, always a gathering site for catbirds and brown thrashers when the berries ripen over the summer. You'll also see magnificent holly trees and pass a large clump of poison ivy (look but don't touch) among the beautiful white sand dunes.

From Toms River, take NJ-37 east across Barnegat Bay and turn right, following signs to Island Beach State Park. Take the main park road to the end after stopping at the Aeolium.

As you walk past the Barnegat Beach Buggy Access sign toward the beach, the going will be slow for a while because of the soft sand, but once you reach hard-packed sand along the water's edge, hiking's a snap. Fishermen, who are allowed in this section with four-wheel-drive vehicles, stake out their favorite spots and sometimes land striped bass or bluefish. Sometimes, too, a patient seagull will suddenly swoop down and grab the catch. Watch for the sandpipers; they dart to and fro searching for a meal of sand fleas as the waves retreat.

If you can pull your eyes away from the ocean, you'll no doubt find many treasures at your feet, such as the cast left by a horseshoe crab from one of its fifteen or so molts. This scary-looking crab sports a long, sharp tail, swims upside down, and has five pairs of legs. Their blue blood is important for cancer research studies, and although they're used primarily as lobster bait nowadays, they were once caught for use as fertilizer and chicken feed. You may also find jingle shells, oysters, or the quahog, used by the Indians for beads and wampum.

The dunes to the right are created by the never-ending wind carrying sand. Examine them carefully (walking on the dunes is not permitted), and you'll find old beach grass, which can survive the driest season because its leaves have the ability to roll up tightly when water is scarce. This grass not only has pretty yellow flowers in the spring, but helps to stablilize the dunes by spreading horizontal roots beneath the sand. Eventually, the roots' stems—called rhizomes—shoot up through the sand every few inches, putting out new plants. In this area are also black cherry, prickly pear cactus, magnolia, trumpet vine, and beach plum.

In the 1750s, Island Beach was known as Cranberry Inlet and was part of an island created when the sea opened a sliver between the ocean and Barnegat Bay (near the northern end of the park). During the 1780s, shipping was a big industry here, and Barnegat Bay was used by the New Jersey Privateers, a group sanctioned by the government to raid British ships. To lure vessels ashore, these pirates would tie a lantern onto an animal's back and lead it along the dunes parallel to the coast. An unsuspecting captain, thinking it was another vessel, would turn toward the light. As soon as the vessel ran aground, the pirates would grab its valuables.

A series of storms closed the inlet in 1812, but life went on

Hikers get more than fresh air and great views on this hike—they have the opportunity to collect choice shells.

peacefully for the two farmers who raised livestock on the land and grew cranberries in the boggy areas. After the lifesaving service was established to aid distressed ships, speculators attempted to promote the land as a dream resort. In 1910 squatters erected shacks in an effort to cash in on a new seaweed industry. Each would collect eelgrass by boat from the shallow waters of Barnegat Bay, hang it to dry, pick it clean of clinging crabs and shrimp, and dry it in the open to get rid of any odor. Afterward, it would be shipped to the mainland for use as mattress stuffing and insulation. Eelgrass was even used inside the upholstery in the Model T Ford! Disease finally wiped out the supply, but today the grass is alive and well once again.

Thanks to Francis Freeman, the beach is here for everyone to enjoy. Freeman took over management of the Phipps estate in 1929 and preserved its natural beauty, according to park officials, by allowing only certain people to enter: those who followed his rules of "no berry picking, dune destruction, littering, and reckless plundering of natural resources." He also allowed a few squatters to lease sections, provided they paid an annual fee to the Phipps estate. However, when the War Department took over in the 1940s, they forced everyone to leave while they worked on antiaircraft rocketry. These efforts led to the launching of a supersonic ramjet rocket in 1945 that traveled over 9 miles at one and one-half times the speed of sound. The property was purchased in 1953 by the state and various fishermen's groups so that the natural beauty of Island Beach would be preserved.

 At 1.5 miles, you'll reach the jetty. Use caution if you walk onto the jetty to watch the fishermen; it's slippery from the spray and moss. Directly across Barnegat Inlet is a landmark in these parts, the Barnegat Lighthouse. When you're finished enjoying the action at this end—the scuba divers, birds, and sandcastle builders—turn back the way you came to the parking area.

---

69. The Plains

Type: Dayhike
Difficulty: Moderate for children
Distance: 4.9 miles, round trip
Elevation gain: Negligible
Hikable: Year-round
Hours: Dawn to dusk
Information: Penn State Park, c/o Bass River State Forest, 762 State Road, New Gretna 08224; (609) 296-1114
Admission: Free

When the colonists first came upon the dwarf trees of the Pine Barrens, they assumed—because none were higher than 5 feet tall—that they had entered a forest of immature trees. However, after all these years, the trees still haven't grown. As you hike into the Plains section of the Pine Barrens, you'll be standing taller than even the tallest tree!

Some theories why these pitch pines remain stunted include poor and acidic soil, toxic ground minerals, and constant wind. A recent theory is that, because the soil surface is always dry and the pines are instant fuel, the frequent fires in this area have kept the trees dwarfed. Fortunately, these pines have a thick bark and the ability to sprout new needles from dormant buds on the trunk and branches. In addition to the stunted trees, you'll have an opportunity to spot white-tailed deer in unusual terrain that boasts 800 different plant species, 91 butterfly species, and 23 types of orchid.

This tour through the Pine Barrens goes along sand roads. Although the map shows names for all of them, not a single one along the route has a sign of any kind. It's a good idea to have a compass along to check directions with those on the map. All roads are open to traffic, and an occasional vehicle may pass by. It's wise to stay to the side of the road and listen for the rumble of an engine. Access to the starting point is via a sand road, generally passable by car. Check driving conditions before entering this road.

From Chatsworth, drive 7 miles south on NJ-563, past the Pine Barrens Canoe Rental, and turn left on a paved road opposite a cardinal-embellished mailbox. Turn left just past the dam impounding Lake Oswego on unmarked Sooey Road (sand). Continue for 1.8 miles and turn right on the side road to Bear Swamp Hill, and park in the lot.

After parking, walk up a few yards to the top of Bear Swamp Hill. Here, standing next to concrete pillars—evidence of a former fire station that was destroyed when a plane crashed through its tower—

A hiker stands taller than the full-grown pines in the heart of the Plains section of the Pine Barrens.

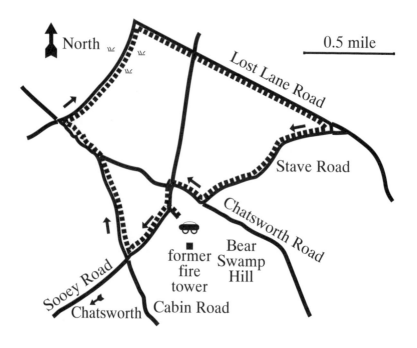

you'll have a bird's-eye view of the pitch pine and oak forest 150 feet below.

Hike down along the entrance road to the fork at 0.1 mile and turn left onto the wide, level sand road. Occasionally an oak pops up amid the tall, thin pines, or you might see a pine snake, which makes its presence known by making a loud hiss and vibrating its tail. Although it acts bravely by flattening its head and puffing its body, this nonpoisonous snake is all show; look it straight in the eye and it will instantly go limp.

Turn right onto Cabin Road at 0.5 mile and follow it to the T, turning left onto Chatsworth Road at about 1 mile, then right onto Lost Lane Road at 1.3 miles going northeastward. The sand, accented by fallen pine needles, is very fine and white along this section. Hawks frequent the cedar swamp section 0.5 mile ahead. Follow the road as it curves to the right in another 0.3 mile.

The dwarf pines in the Plains appear at 2.6 miles. There is something eerie about the wind whistling through the stunted trees. Along the sides of the road are low-bush blueberry. You may also see deer tracks. Turn right at the Y onto Stave Road (3.6 miles) and then right again on Chatsworth Road at the T a mile later. At the crossroad, turn left on Sooey Road and then left again up to Bear Swamp Hill, the starting point.

70. Batsto Lake

Type: Dayhike
Difficulty: Easy for children
Distance: 2.2 miles, round trip
Elevation gain: Negligible
Hikable: Year-round; usually crowded in summer
Hours: Trail, dawn to dusk; village, daily Memorial Day through Labor Day, 10:00 A.M.–5:00 P.M.; 10:00 A.M.–4:00 P.M. the rest of the year
Information: c/o Wharton State Forest, Batsto, RD 9, Hammonton 08037; (609) 561-3262
Admission: Parking fee from Memorial Day through Labor Day

You won't get "bogged down" hiking along the perimeter of Batsto Lake, where you can have fun bouncing up and down on the spongy sphagnum moss found in the boggy areas. Look closely to find insect-trapping pitcher plants and sundews, as well as British soldiers, the tiny scarlet lichens named for the "redcoats" of the Revolutionary War. White sand, red oaks, cedars, and towering pitch pines make this a delightful hike. The trail is very narrow and overgrown with greenbrier in some areas, so long sleeves and pants are recommended. When you're finished hiking, explore historic Batsto Village, where an iron furnace operated over 200 years ago.

From the Garden State Parkway exit at New Gretna, take NJ-542 west 12.5 miles to Batsto Village.

Walk southwest from the information center toward the ironmaster's mansion, turning right onto a gravel road at the information map. Follow the sign for the Sawmill Nature Center at 0.1 mile, and turn right at the lake along a flat, sandy trail. With the lake on the left, turn left at a wooden-rail fence at about 0.3 mile, onto the yellow-blazed Pond Trail. Although markings may be missing or hidden by foliage, the path is usually easy to follow. You'll immediately see stands of pitch pine, a cone-bearing evergreen with long, thick needles always in clusters of three. Here too is the sassafras sporting mitten-shaped leaves. Oil from its roots is used in flavoring root beer

The ironmaster's mansion at the beginning of the trail

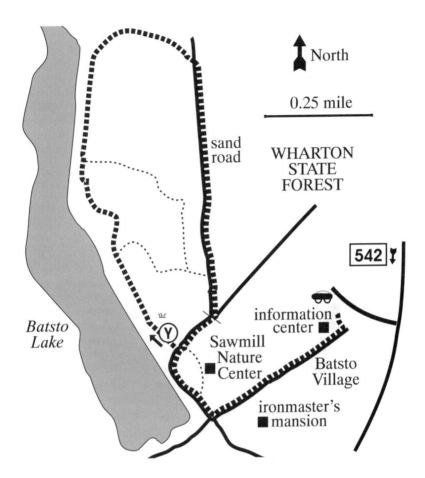

and various medicines. From May to July, check the wet areas for the delicate pink lady's slipper. Admire, but don't touch, this member of the orchid family. (Touching the hairs covering the stem of this rare plant may cause a skin reaction.)

The trail narrows after a short boardwalk, and greenbrier thorns reach out unexpectedly from the brush. Just when you think the trail will swallow you completely, it widens again. A good view of Batsto Lake, which was formed in 1766 when the Batsto River was dammed, appears at 0.6 mile. Water from this manmade lake was harnessed to provide power for the sawmill and iron furnace when the village was in its prime. A few yards farther is a bog rich in sphagnum moss and carnivorous plants, such as the sundew and pitcher plants. Spend a few minutes at the wide clearing at the water's edge in about another 0.5 mile to study the skeletons of southern white cedar destroyed by a fire in 1960. Today, they're sprouting new growth from scattered windblown seed.

When the trail turns away from the lake at a wide area at about 1.25 miles, bear right into the woods, following the pale yellow blaze. Turn right at the T on the sand road at 1.4 miles. As you walk through this lovely oak and pine forest, you'll get plenty of exercise because the sand is very deep and soft. In 0.5 mile, walk around the fence and continue straight ahead. The lake comes into view again on the right at just under 2 miles. In a few yards you'll be passing where you originally turned off; retrace your steps back to the start or stop to explore the village.

Note: Camping is available at several sites within Wharton State Forest. Check at the visitor center for further details.

Dragonfly

Besides the ocean, birds, and Atlantic City's skyline, Holgate hikers can see anglers trying for dinner.

71. Holgate

Type:	Dayhike
Difficulty:	Easy for children
Distance:	4.7 miles, round trip
Elevation gain:	None
Hikable:	Year-round, except during nesting season from Apr. 1– Aug. 31 (subject to change; call before going)
Hours:	None
Information:	Refuge Manager, Edwin B. Forsythe National Wildlife Refuge, P.O. Box 72, Great Creek Road, Oceanville 08231; (609) 652-1665
Admission:	Free

You might not notice it unless you return year after year, but the beach at Holgate is constantly shifting under the influence of changing tides and sporadic storms. This 2.5-mile strip, located at the south end of Long Beach Island, is part of the Edwin B. Forsythe National

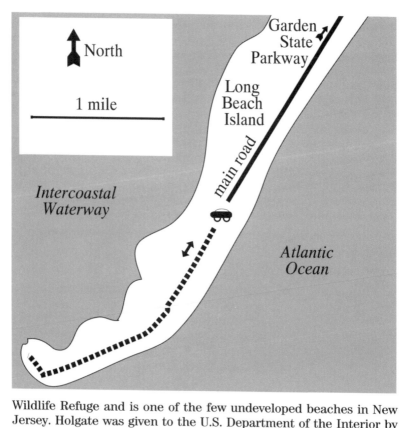

Wildlife Refuge and is one of the few undeveloped beaches in New Jersey. Holgate was given to the U.S. Department of the Interior by the National Audubon Society in 1960.

Hiking with pounding surf on one side and large dunes on the other is a tonic for the soul. Arrive a couple of hours before sunset to watch the sky suddenly come ablaze just as the lights go on in Atlantic City's gambling casinos across the water. Bring a pair of binoculars; this is prime nesting territory for three birds on New Jersey's endangered species list—the piping plover, the black skimmer, and the least tern. You won't be allowed to roam near the nests, but during summer months you can watch the birds in flight, along with the peregrine falcon, glossy ibis, snowy egret, and other beauties. If you're not a birdwatcher, hike here after a storm; you may find a Spanish coin left by pirates. Or simply enjoy the fresh air and sand dunes, and the sight of a fisherman landing dinner.

From Exit 63 on the Garden State Parkway, take NJ-72 east and go straight onto Long Beach Island. Turn right on the main street and follow it for about 9 miles to a parking lot at the end.

Atlantic City's skyline is visible in the distance as you walk onto the beach from the parking area. At the water's edge sandpipers chase the retreating waves. That harsh cry you'll probably hear is from a laughing gull hovering overhead. On the way to the point, keep an eye open for a pretty shell, such as the Atlantic moon snail or blood ark shells. If you see jets of water spurting out of the sand during low tide, dig down quickly and you may find a soft-shell clam. Round the point (at 2.25 miles) and continue walking for about another 0.25 mile. Other sections of the refuge stretch out before you across the bay. During winter this is where the great black-backed gull, the largest gull on the East Coast, hangs out. It sports a white head and breast, black wings and back, and a yellow bill.

When you're ready, return to the parking area the way you came.

72. Brigantine Island

Type:	Dayhike
Difficulty:	Easy for children
Distance:	5 miles, round trip
Elevation gain:	None
Hikable:	Year-round
Hours:	None
Information:	Refuge Manager, Edwin B. Forsythe National Wildlife Refuge, P.O. Box 72, Great Creek Road, Oceanville 08231; (609) 652-1665
Admission:	Free

If you haven't had any luck at the casinos, you may strike it rich hiking along the flat, well-packed sands at Brigantine Island. Maybe you won't find the leather-and-brass chest Captain Kidd buried here in 1698, but there are other gems waiting to be discovered. These include the long, narrow Atlantic jackknife clam, strings of knobbed whelk egg capsules, and an assortment of shellfish found beneath rocks, planks, and driftwood.

From Exit 40 on the Garden State Parkway, take NJ-30 east. Turn left on NJ-87 and follow it to a parking area at the end.

Walk onto the beach and you'll immediately feel the invigorating effect of the fresh salt air and the roaring surf. Walk briskly so there will be time to beachcomb. (A plastic bag comes in handy for carrying shells.) Old pilings, lined up in an interesting pattern, are at 1.25 miles. A short distance before the point, to the northeast, are treacherous sandbars.

When you reach Brigantine Inlet at 2.5 miles, you'll see why fishing boats keep their distance; more than 300 vessels have been wrecked on the shoals in this area since the late 1700s. In 1849, a Scottish ship carrying 200 passengers hit a bar. Fortunately, it was equipped with a newly perfected breeches buoy—a device consisting of a pair of breeches within a floating ring. Using this, people could be rescued

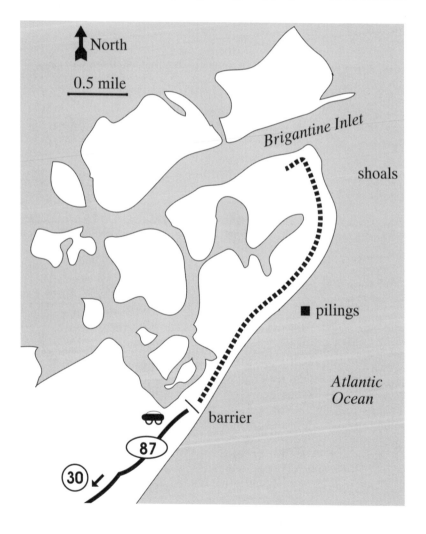

one by one via a line extending from the ship to shore. Other ships, however, weren't as lucky; in 1854, the *Powhaten* broke in half, taking all aboard down with her.

Into the early 1800s, parts of the island were only accessible by sailboat and later by scheduled motorboat. Thanks to a new trolley line, visitors began coming to see the dunes in 1892, but it wasn't until the $10 million bridge was erected in 1972 that the area became popular. James Baremore, the island's first official resident in 1802, liked the surroundings so much that he erected a home right on the beach. Once, during the War of 1812, a British war party raided his garden, but his twelve-year-old son convinced the soldiers to pay for the vegetables. Because of sand erosion, the house vanished into the sea long ago.

Continue walking as far as you like before turning around and returning the way you came. Good timing will bring hikers to the island a couple of hours before sunset; with luck, the sun will disappear and set the sky aglow with vibrant colors during the return leg. There's nothing quite as beautiful as watching a full moon rise over the ocean as the western sky glows a brilliant red. If you're here in the evening, you'll also see the lights of Atlantic City go on across the water.

Sharing treasures found while hiking along the sands of Brigantine Island

73. Parvin State Park

Type:	Dayhike or overnight camping
Difficulty:	Easy for children
Distance:	3 miles, round trip
Elevation gain:	Negligible
Hikable:	Year-round; fall and winter are best
Hours:	Dawn to dusk
Information:	Parvin State Park, 701 Almond Road, Pittsgrove 08318; (856) 358-8616
Admission:	Free; fee for parking Memorial Day through Labor Day and for camping

Parvin State Park is a product of the 1930s. The campground and trails were built by young men in the Civilian Conservation Corps (CCC) who lived in army-style barracks in the middle of the woods. The work was hard and the hours long, but the men were grateful to earn a few dollars to send to their families during the Depression. Few realized they'd soon be serving their country in another way, during World War II. Eventually, the barracks they built in Parvin were used to house German prisoners of war.

If they hiked this 1,125-acre forest today, they'd no doubt be proud of their accomplishment. Much of the park has been dedicated as a

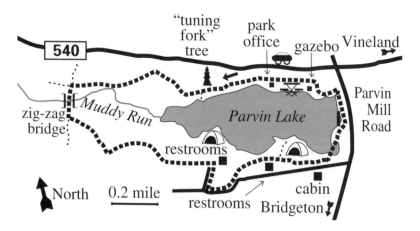

natural area, with trails leading through a variety of habitats. These include cedar swamps, pine forests, and holly groves with lush patches of mountain laurel. Parvin boasts 123 species of birds, as well as an abundance of deer, salamanders, toads, and turtles. Along with over 200 herbaceous flowering plants, the opportunity to swim in Parvin Lake and a profusion of club mosses and ferns carpeting the forest floor make the hike a winner.

Camping is available on Jaggers Point (along the south shore of Parvin Lake), and cabins may be rented on the north shore of Thundergust Lake. It's best to come during fall or winter so that the mosquitos don't carry you away, and to wear long pants and sleeves year-round to protect against ticks.

From Vineland take NJ-540 west about 6 miles. Park in the lot opposite the park office.

Facing the office, turn right onto the hard-packed sand trail so that Parvin Lake is to your left and County Road 540 to your right. Tall hollies appear immediately. In winter, their thick green spiny-tipped leaves and brilliant red berries stand out against a backdrop of snow. These are followed by pitch pines, which provide a fine bed of needles, while erect mosses hold their heads high beneath the fragrant canopy. You'll come to a tree with a tuning fork–shaped trunk at about 0.3 mile. Directly behind it is a chunky pitch pine, identifiable by its three-to-a-bundle curved needles. If you touch one of the buds or branches, a sticky substance will ooze out, the pitch of its name. A short distance ahead is an opening in the woods and an unmarked trail junction; bear right. The woods are filled with hollies and a few red maples and sweet gums. Turn left at the junction at 0.8 mile, following the wide paved trail to Muddy Run, a pleasant stream that empties into Delaware Bay. Cross over the zigzag bridge, a popular spot for birding, and continue on a very wide track for a few yards. Turn left, just past an impressive cedar stand, onto a narrow, sandy trail beneath pines. Watch out for the greenbrier. In a few yards, you'll cross over a stream on a few planks and will enter the natural area.

There are a few ups and downs, but they're hardly noticeable. The campground appears at 1.5 miles. At the restrooms and bathhouse, turn right, walking straight on the auto road, which is usually lightly traveled. New pine growth is apparent off to the side.

At the stop sign and Jaggers Point Campsite sign, turn left, but exercise caution, staying to the left and facing oncoming cars. After passing a set of posts on the left, proceed to the second set of posts at 1.9 miles, and turn left onto the sand trail, which makes a slight dip into the woods for a few feet and then levels. At the junction just ahead turn right, passing the cedar, mountain laurel, and holly that flank the trail on both sides.

Parvin Lake is soon visible on the left. This is another great place for bird observation. At an opening, continue straight ahead, keeping the group campsite to the left and the restroom to the right. The sandy trail passes a log cabin before reaching a boat ramp and a good place to view the lake again. Turn left and cross the bridge. A few minutes' walk reveals a close-up view of the horseshoe-shaped dam from its retaining wall. Walk around the dam and cross the small bridge, heading toward the picturesque gazebo ahead, onto the wide, open lawn area. Ducks and geese can usually be seen lazing about in this section. You'll reach a narrow trail heading into the woods again, with a picnic area on the left by the lake. Keep going a bit more and you'll reach your car.

74. Belleplain Circular

Type:	Dayhike or overnight camping
Difficulty:	Moderate
Distance:	4.9 miles, round trip
Elevation gain:	Negligible
Hikable:	Year-round; fall and winter are best
Hours:	Dawn to dusk
Information:	Belleplain State Forest, Box 450, Woodbine 08270; (609) 861-2404
Admission:	Free; fee for parking Memorial Day through Labor Day and for camping

Chief Nummy and his tribe hiked through this southernmost area of the state many times. Some of that area has been protected as Belleplain State Forest and Pinelands Preserve. What mattered to the Indians was the excellent hunting and fishing in this area, and today you can still find white-tailed deer, red foxes, and ruffed grouse here, as well as a variety of fish in the lake. Lake Nummy, named for the chief, is the starting point for this hike.

Hiking deeper into the woods you'll find trees typical of the coastal plain, including pitch pine, black and white oak, and American holly. In the low swamp areas, magnificent stands of Atlantic white cedar stretch toward the sky, and red-bellied turtles and frogs stretch out on logs during their rest breaks. Bring a magnifying glass for a close-up look at sphagnum moss and cinnamon fern, or binoculars for spotting

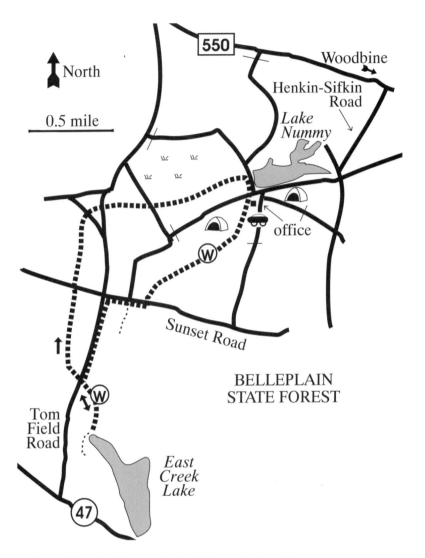

birds as they dart in and out of the underbrush.

A swim in Lake Nummy is just the ticket after hiking on a hot day, but it's best to come during fall or winter to minimize exposure to mosquitos and ticks. Wear long sleeves and pants year-round to safeguard against overgrown shrubs. Although this hike is on fairly level trails, be prepared to exert a great deal of energy in places where the sandy trail is soft.

From the town of Woodbine in northern Cape May County take NJ-550 west toward Belleplain and turn left on Henkin-Sifkin Road, then right at the entrance to Belleplain State Forest. Park on the left next to the office, opposite Lake Nummy.

Walk onto the paved road in front of the forest office, a small log building, toward the sign for group sites, and turn left at the wood lot at 0.1 mile. A white blaze on a tree on the right leads into the woods beneath a canopy of pine and oak. Stands of mountain laurel appear at 0.5 mile. This section of the trail is easy walking. At 0.9 mile, towering red-trunked cedars covered with bright green lichens appear. Immediately after crossing the short boardwalk ahead, watch for tree roots that have spread across the trail. Sunset Road, a paved auto road, is just ahead. Pause to examine the scrub oaks that grow at this intersection. You'll find dozens of ball-shaped galls, evidence that insects have adopted a leaf or branch as their home. After an insect has landed, the tree, aggravated by the invasion, oozes a substance around the culprit which, in turn, forms the fragile ball casing.

Turn right onto the pavement, walking opposite the light traffic. Impressive stands of mountain laurel are on the left side of the road, and at 1.1 miles a pretty brook flows beneath the bridge. This is an excellent place to wait for deer or see birds, especially chickadees. Turn left onto Tom Field Road, a wide sand road, at 1.25 miles, and continue for just over 0.5 mile until white blazes appear on trees on both sides of the road. Turn left into the woods. Almost immediately, you'll have to duck under mountain laurel with thick, gnarled branches.

A short walk leads to the edge of East Creek Lake, a serene, watery oasis surrounded by woods. Ducks and geese usually hang out here, and, with luck, a deer may choose to come to the water's edge for a drink. When you've drunk your fill of the beautiful scene, turn around and follow the white blazes back, crossing the sand road into the woods. The trail, a narrow, meandering path, soon leads through a jungle of mountain laurel. After clearing this obstacle, oak, red maple, and a scattering of holly take over, followed by a pine grove at 3 miles. Use caution when crossing Sunset Road. After another 0.5 mile through woods, cross two sand roads before entering lovely holly and cedar stands.

A short boardwalk in the wet area at 3.7 miles helps keep feet dry, despite the fact that many of the boards are under water. Sphagnum moss is very much in evidence beneath the cedars. Pitch pine dominate on slightly higher ground 0.1 mile later, with a hemlock popping up every so often. One-half mile after crossing a blacktop road, the trail reaches a cedar swamp. Pause for a few minutes. Children will love examining this boggy area. Lake Nummy, a former cranberry bog that was dug out in the 1930s by the Civilian Conservation Corps, is just ahead. Today, its western tip serves as a bathing beach, while boaters and fishermen also take advantage of this small, but enjoyable lake. Turn right and walk back to your car.

Hikers deep in the woods of Belleplain State Forest

75. Diamond Beach

Type:	Dayhike
Difficulty:	Moderate for children
Distance:	2.5 miles, round trip
Elevation gain:	Negligible
Hikable:	Year-round
Hours:	Dawn to dusk
Information:	Higbee Beach Wildlife Management Area, New Jersey Dept. of Environmental Protection, Division of Fish and Wildlife, CN400, Trenton 08625-0400; (609) 292-2965
Admission:	Free

Diamonds are forever—that is, unless they're Cape May diamonds. These ersatz gems, found along several Delaware Bay beaches, are actually quartz pebbles that have been broken up and deposited on the sands by thousands of years of waves. At one time, there were so many of these "diamonds" on Higbee Beach that it was called "Diamond Beach."

Other gems encountered on this hike include dense woods, meadows, and towering white sand dunes. While many serious birdwatchers flock to the tip of nearby Cape May, which is world-famous for the fall bird migration, you'll be able to spot many of the same birds without the crowds. Over 250 species are present at Higbee Beach Wildlife Management Area, including the bald eagle.

The hike is short, but trudging through the mushy sand can sometimes be tiring. Allow extra time to linger while examining driftwood and pretty shells along the beach. While you can refresh yourself by dipping your feet into Delaware Bay during warm weather, don't swim; there aren't any lifeguards, but there is a strong undertow.

 From West Cape May, take County Route 607 (Bay Shore Road) north. Turn left at the junction with NJ-641, continuing to the parking lot at the end of the road. Parking is permitted here after Labor Day to a week before Memorial Day. Other times, park in authorized lots only along New England Road.

A number of unmarked trails originate at the parking area. Walk to the left of the information board and take the trail heading west, into the woods. At the first fork, bear left, then make a second left a few feet later onto a narrow, level path beneath a canopy of oak, holly, and bayberry. Keep an eye peeled for the cottontail rabbit, a cute critter sporting a fluffy white tail, or the amazing woodcock, which has the ability to detect predators in any direction thanks to enormous eyes set way back in its head.

At the T, bear right onto a wide trail leading to a meadow dominated by common reed and flanked on both sides by dense woods. Occasional yellow blazes define the route. The trail narrows, briefly passes through woods, and, just before it widens again where a pole sports a yellow blaze, continues through another small meadow. Turn right, into the woods, at the yellow blaze at 0.5 mile. Follow the yellow markers as the trail makes several quick turns before reaching the dune area. It's difficult trudging through the soft sand, but you probably won't mind the exertion as you pass the beautiful beach plum, honeysuckle, and Virginia creeper found throughout the dune area. These plants help to keep the fragile dunes in place.

At about 0.75 mile, with the trail heading in a northerly direction, you'll hear the roar of the surf. Look to the left for a great view of Delaware Bay, which is so vast that many mistake it for the Atlantic Ocean. A good spot to detour down to the beach lies a few yards ahead. Higbee Beach is loaded with driftwood and shells, especially after a storm. Children are usually fascinated by the huge discarded shells the horseshoe crab leaves behind after each molt, and if they turn it over, they'll see how closely the rim resembles a horseshoe. Zoologists describe this creature as a living fossil with good reason: It dates back over 300 million years to the Triassic period. Growing up to 20 inches, it swims upside down. It's also blue-blooded; that's because its blood contains copper instead of iron, and turns blue when exposed to oxygen.

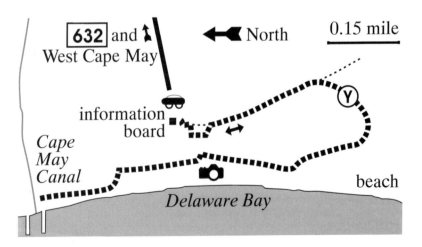

Driftwood is only one of the treasures to be found on the hike along Higbee Beach, once known as "Diamond Beach."

Continue on the trail past shrub oak and seaside goldenrod. After a series of ups and downs along soft sand, you'll reach the end of the trail at about 1 mile. At this point, walk to the left onto Higbee Beach. This is a good spot for beachcombing. Walk to the right toward the jetty of the Cape May Canal. From the beach, you can watch ferries ply the waters of Delaware Bay, or be entertained by the aerial performances put on by birds free of charge. You'll probably have a difficult time leaving this spot when children are searching the sand for interesting shells and the famous diamonds.

Higbee Beach extends 1.5 miles south from this point toward Sunset Boulevard. During the summer, it's 30 yards deep, but in winter months the beach narrows due to tidal action that causes erosion. If you look to the left, you'll see what appears to be a blob of concrete in the distance. That's the 3,000-ton *Atlantus,* which is, indeed, a huge piece of concrete. One of fourteen experimental vessels built by the government during World War I, and used for a short time as a coal steamer, it was towed here after it began to sink in a storm in 1926.

When ready, return to the parking area the way you came.

Horseshoe crab molt looks like the real "monster."

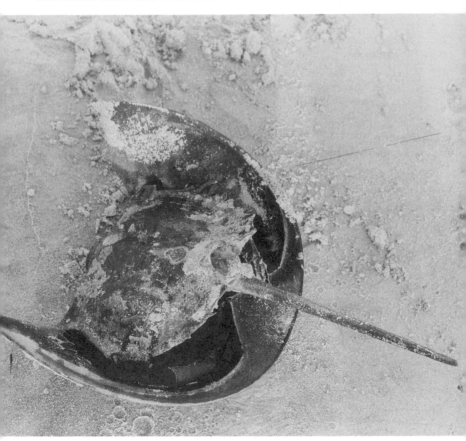

Appendix

ORGANIZATIONS

American Hiking Society, 1422 Fenwick Lane, Silver Spring, MD 20910

Appalachian Mountain Club, 5 Joy Street, Boston, MA 02108

New York–New Jersey Trail Conference, 156 Ramapo Valley Road, Mahwah, NJ 07430

Sierra Club, National Headquarters, 85 Second Street, San Francisco, CA 94105

Union County Hiking Club, Division of Parks and Recreation, Administration Building, Elizabeth, NJ 07207-2204

RECOMMENDED BOOKS

Blandford, Percy W. *Maps and Compasses: A User's Handbook*. Summit, PA: Tab Books, 1984. Learn how to read a map, a compass, and the sun and stars, and never get lost.

Brown, Robert E. *Emergency/Survival Handbook*. Seattle: The Mountaineers Books, 1987. This pocket-sized book offers quick-indexed information for outdoor medical emergencies, and can be used as a signaling device or fire starter.

Collins, Henry Hill. *Complete Field Guide to North American Wildlife*. New York: Harper & Row, 1981. Excellent illustrations and a very complete reference guide.

Coulombe, Sarah A. *The Seaside Naturalist*. New York: Prentice-Hall Press, 1984. Filled with a wealth of information for beachcombers, animal lovers, and amateur naturalists.

Day, John A., and Vincent J. Schaefer. *Peterson First Guides: Clouds and Weather*. Boston: Houghton Mifflin, 1991. Compact guide showing how to identify clouds, with explanations of what each cloud type tells about approaching weather.

Durrell, Gerald. *A Practical Guide for the Amateur Naturalist*. New York: Knopf, 1986. An introduction to the natural world, with suggestions on everything from constructing a blind to starting collections, plus color illustrations.

Hayman, Peter, et al. *Shorebirds*. Boston: Houghton Mifflin, 1986. A complete identification guide to the waders and shorebirds of the world, with color plates and detailed maps.

Hunken, Jorie. *Botany for All Ages*. Chester, CT: Globe Pequot Press, 1989. An easy-to-read introduction to botany for all ages.

Marchand, Peter J. *North Woods*. Boston: Appalachian Mountain Club, 1987. A compact guide, with illustrations for plant identification, and more.

Martin, Laura C. *Wildflower Folklore*. Chester, CT: Globe Pequot, 1984. Delightful descriptions and folklore relating to wildflowers.

National Wildlife Federation. *The Unhuggables*. Washington, DC: National Wildlife Federation, 1988. Scary and pesty critters have interesting lives, and this beautifully illustrated book will bare their secrets to you.

Peattie, Donald C. *A Natural History of Trees of Eastern and Central North America*. Boston: Houghton Mifflin, 1991. A detailed handbook with clear descriptions and full historical information covering all of the native American trees of the region.

Peterson, Lee Allen. *A Field Guide to Edible Wild Plants*. Boston: Houghton Mifflin, 1977. A detailed field guide to edible wild plants found in fourteen habitats, including food uses and preparation tips.

Peterson, Roger Tory, et al. *A Field Guide to the Birds*. Boston: Houghton Mifflin, 1980. For identifying the chirping source overhead.

Peterson, Roger Tory, et al. *A Field Guide to Wildflowers of Northeastern North America*. Boston: Houghton Mifflin, 1974. Most helpful during spring in figuring out the bright carpet of wildflowers at your feet.

Petrides, George A. *A Field Guide to Trees and Shrubs*. Boston: Houghton Mifflin, 1973. Perfect for easy identification along the trail.

Petry, Loren C. *A Beachcomber's Botany*. Chatham, MA: The Chatham Conservation Foundation, Inc., 1982. Flora identification through drawings.

Robbins, Chandler S., et al. *Birds of North America*. New York: Golden Press, 1983. Great for figuring out the song you hear above.

Silver, Donald M., and Patricia J. Wynne. *The Checkerboard Press Nature Encyclopedia*. New York: Checkerboard Press, 1990. Information and full-color drawings in a comprehensive encyclopedia of nature subjects for third to sixth graders.

Steele, Frederic L. *At Timberline, A Nature Guide to the Mountains of the Northeast*. Boston: Appalachian Mountain Club, 1982. Brief descriptions and precise illustrations for on-the-spot identification of birds, mammals, reptiles, amphibians, wildflowers, geologic formations, trees, ferns, and grasses.

Zinn, Donald. *The Handbook for Beach Strollers*. Chester, CT: Globe Pequot, 1985. A discovery guide for learning how to explore the rocky and sandy Atlantic shores.

INFORMATION ON NEW JERSEY

Adams, Arthur G. *The Hudson Through The Years*. Westwood, NJ: Lind Publications, 1983. Clearly narrated.

Cunningham, John T. *This Is New Jersey*. New Brunswick, NJ: Rutgers University Press, 1978. A guide to the state's history, towns, historic sites, and counties.

Lawrence, Susanna, and Barbara Gross. *Audubon Society Field Guide to the Natural Places of the Mid-Atlantic States (Inland)*. New York: Random House, 1984. Maps, tours, and descriptions of places for the nature lover.

McPhee, John. *The Pine Barrens*. New York: Ballantine Books, 1990. A journey into the southern part of the state.

Menzies, Elizabeth G. C. *Passage Between Rivers*. New Brunswick, NJ: Rutgers University Press, 1976. An enjoyable history of the Delaware & Raritan Canal.

Pierce, Arthur D. *Iron in the Pines*. New Brunswick, NJ: Rutgers University Press, 1957. History of iron manufacturing in southern New Jersey.

Scofield, Bruce, et al. *Circuit Hikes in Northern New Jersey*. New York: New York–New Jersey Trail Conference, 1987. Short descriptions of northern hikes.

Stember, Sol. *Bicentennial Guide to the American Revolution*. New York: Dutton, 1974. The history of the Middle Colonies and Revolutionary War sites is presented in volume II.

Various. *New York Walk Book*. New York: New York–New Jersey Trail Conference, 1984. Maps and descriptions of geological and natural history of the region.

Zatz, Arline. *New Jersey's Special Places*. Woodstock, VT: The Countryman Press, 1998. More than fifty-two detailed outings in New Jersey's most fascinating natural and historical places.

Zatz, Arline. *30 Bicycle Tours in New Jersey*. Woodstock, VT: Backcountry Publications, 1998. Informative descriptions of the outstanding natural, cultural, and historic features encountered in the Garden State, along with tours ranging from a couple of hours to overnight.

STATE CAMPGROUNDS

Allaire State Park, Box 220, Farmingdale 07727; (732) 938-2371

Allamuchy Mountain State Park, Stephen's Section, Hackettstown 07840; (908) 852-3790

Bass River State Forest, Stage Road, P.O. Box 118, New Gretna 08824; (609) 296-1114

Belleplain State Forest, Box 450, Woodbine 08270; (609) 861-2404

Bull's Island Section, Delaware & Raritan Canal State Park, 2185 Daniel Bray Highway (Route 29), Stockton 08559; (609) 397-2949

Cheesequake State Park, 300 Gordon Road, Matawan 07747; (732) 566-2161

High Point State Park, 1480 State Route 23, Sussex 07461; (973) 875-4800

Jenny Jump State Forest, P.O. Box 150, Hope 07844; (908) 459-4366

Lebanon State Forest, P.O. Box 215, New Lisbon 08064; (609) 726-1191

Parvin State Park, 701 Almond Road, Pittsgrove 08318; (856) 358-8616

Round Valley Recreation Area, Box 45D, Lebanon-Stanton Road, Lebanon 08833; (908) 236-6355

Spruce Run Recreation Area, 289 Van Syckels Road, Clinton 08809; (908) 638-8572

Stokes State Forest, 1 Coursen Road, Branchville 07826; (973) 948-3820

Swartswood State Park, P.O. Box 123, Swartswood 07877; (973) 383-5230

Voorhees State Park, 251 County Road, Route 513, Glen Gardner 08826; (908) 638-6969

Wawayanda State Park, 885 Warwick Turnpike, Hewitt 07421; (973) 853-4462

Wharton State Forest, 4110 Nesco Road, Hammonton 08037; (609) 561-3262

Worthington State Forest, HC62, Box 2, Columbia 07832; (908) 841-9575

For a listing of private campgrounds, consult the Trailer Life *RV Campground & Services Directory*. Ventura, CA: TL Enterprises, and the KOA *Kampgrounds Directory*. Billings, MT: Kampgrounds of America.

Index

About Arline Zatz and Joel Zatz:

Writer/photographer Arline Zatz "knows New Jersey like no other," exclaims a leading New Jersey newspaper. *Best Hikes With Children in New Jersey* is her third book about the Garden State; the first, *25 Bicycle Tours in New Jersey,* was written with her husband, Joel Zatz. She is also the author of *New Jersey's Special Places,* which was judged to be the best non-fiction book of the year by both the National Federation of Press Women and the North American Travel Journalist Association, and *30 Bicycle Tours in New Jersey.* Ms. Zatz was named Travel Writer of the Year by the Pennsylvania Travel Council in 1985. Her writing and photography has appeared in *The New York Times,* the *Asbury Park Press,* the *Star-Ledger,* the *New York Daily News,* and *New Jersey Outdoors Magazine,* among others. Her latest book is *New Jersey's Great Gardens.*

Joel Zatz is the co-author of *25 Bicycle Tours in New Jersey* and a professor of pharmaceutics at Rutgers University. Dr. Zatz, an experienced hiker, outdoorsman, and photographer who has been exploring the New Jersey countryside with his family for many years, researched his favorite hikes for this book.

The MOUNTAINEERS, founded in 1906, is a nonprofit outdoor activity and conservation club, whose mission is "to explore, study, preserve, and enjoy the natural beauty of the outdoors. . . ." Based in Seattle, Washington, the club is now the third-largest such organization in the United States, with 15,000 members and five branches throughout Washington State.

The Mountaineers sponsors both classes and year-round outdoor activities in the Pacific Northwest, which include hiking, mountain climbing, ski-touring, snowshoeing, bicycling, camping, kayaking and canoeing, nature study, sailing, and adventure travel. The club's conservation division supports environmental causes through educational activities, sponsoring legislation, and presenting informational programs. All club activities are led by skilled, experienced volunteers, who are dedicated to promoting safe and responsible enjoyment and preservation of the outdoors.

If you would like to participate in these organized outdoor activities or the club's programs, consider a membership in The Mountaineers. For information and an application, write or call The Mountaineers, Club Headquarters, 300 Third Avenue West, Seattle, Washington 98119; (206) 284-6310.

The Mountaineers Books, an active, nonprofit publishing program of the club, produces guidebooks, instructional texts, historical works, natural history guides, and works on environmental conservation. All books produced by The Mountaineers are aimed at fulfilling the club's mission.

Send or call for our catalog of more than 300 outdoor books:
The Mountaineers Books
1001 SW Klickitat Way, Suite 201
Seattle, WA 98134
1-800-553-4453